Extended World Travel

How to take a break from
the rat race and travel the
world with your family

Maria Berkestam &
Magnus Drysén

Please visit:
www.extendedworldtravel.com

ISBN 978-3-8391-9868-1

Copyright © Maria Berkestam & Magnus Drysén, October 2010
info@extendedworldtravel.com

Cover design by Gabi Reichert

Manufactured and published by Books on Demand GmbH, Norderstedt, Germany

Disclaimer

This book is intended to provide information related to travel. The book is provided with the understanding that the authors and the publisher are not making any claims with regard to the information contained herein. Every effort has been made to offer accurate information with regard to travel and lifestyle but every individual will have different experiences from travel. This text should be used only as a general guide and reference regarding the possibilities of travel and not as an authoritative source.

The authors and the publisher shall have neither liability nor responsibility to any person or entity with respect to any loss or damage caused or alleged to be caused directly or indirectly by the information covered in this Book.

TABLE OF CONTENTS

1. Introduction

"Twenty years from now you will be more disappointed by the things you didn't do than by the ones you did do. So throw off the bowlines, sail away from the safe harbor. Catch the trade winds in your sails. Explore. Dream. Discover."
- Mark Twain

Years ago, we were a family with three young children and, like so many others; our days were full of everyday commitments and stress. We spent our days driving the kids back and forth to school and to different activities, running our own company, renovating the big old house we lived in, trying hard to make both ends meet financially, and find time to really be with each other. But no matter how hard we tried, there never seemed to be enough time for everything, nor enough money.

Finally, we came to a point where we'd had enough. We got rid of the company, our house and the kids' school as well as of a few limiting beliefs, bought an old campervan and started driving. When people asked where we were going, we told them we'd set the compass on south and then just keep driving, and we'd keep going as long as we wanted to.

This, our first long term trip together as a family, turned out to go on for five months and it was like heaven on earth. Well, actually not the whole time. As we had been living at a high level of stress before we left, we brought a lot of that stressful mode with us also along the way. It took time to get used to this new life, and in the beginning, it felt like everything went wrong. The car broke down (and not just once), we all got really sick, not to mention that we got lost time after time in the most unsuitable places. The kids were impatient and the atmosphere stressed and confused (but at times it felt like total freedom).

This went on for the first two months, until one day we found ourselves arriving in Southern Spain, as far away as we had actually planned to go. Now things suddenly changed and we entered a new phase. Our old stressful state was just gone and we settled into something totally different. We felt totally relaxed and were able to just take the days as they came whatever happened. And actually, nothing went "wrong" anymore. The kids played together all the time and we all felt just - happy! We finally had the time to just be and to listen to each other and experience whatever we had around us and what turned up. After the first two months of unwinding from the stress, we went on to have the best time ever.

The rest of our five month trip continued in this happy and relaxed spirit. But it took us two months to get to this new place, both physically and mentally! We have often talked about this – the importance of allowing enough time when you travel and how little an "ordinary" one, two or even a three week vacation can help you to let go of all your everyday stuff and allow you to settle into a new mindset.

Of course, it's always great to take some time off, experience new things and to recharge your batteries. But if you are looking for a more life transforming effect, you usually need a lot more time than the usual short vacation provides. We've heard many other long term travelers say this too, that things start to happen inside you somewhere between six to eight weeks after you've left home. The exact amount of transition time depends on what kind of life you've lived before you left and how stressful it was.

It is actually not until after this transition time that your journey really can begin. And that's why we're not talking about just any travel here, but EXTENDED travel.

Going on that first long journey really changed our lives. We have since been on several other long journeys, both in time and distance and every time it has taken our life in new and better directions.

We believe there are so many benefits from traveling for an extended period of time and that's why we really want to encourage you to create your own long term journey.

2. What Is This Book All About?

Well let's put it this way, the bookstores are full of books telling you about how to travel, about how to pack and how to save money on flights, what to do, what to see and how to find accommodations. It's really not our goal to provide you with a lot of such information, since there are so many others out there probably doing it better.

But how about all of you who are dreaming about going on a long journey but just don't think you can do it? How do you take your dream from "just" a desire and start to make it a reality? How do you overcome the obstacles that prevent you from even seeing that a long journey is possible for you too? What about all the road blocks that turn up before you even get as far as buying that guide book about Brazil, Tanzania or maybe Colorado?

Our intention here is to give answers to questions we've been asked so many times ourselves. Questions which are almost never about cheap hotels or flights, what to see or do or where to go. No, the kinds of questions we get are almost always about what we do *before* we can take off in the first place. Like how we make room for a long journey in our busy life. How we get the money to travel around the world for an extended period or what we do with the kids school or with our jobs. And, of course, people also ask us why we travel and live the life we do and how this could be possible for them as well.

So, these are the kind of things we want to share with you and we also wish to help you get clearer about why you should, and how you could, make a reality of that old dream of traveling the world.

After having followed us through this book, you'll have found answers to questions like:

- Why should you travel in the first place? Why do you have the desire? What are you really dreaming about?
- Why would traveling be good for you? What will you gain from taking time off to travel? Most people think traveling is just about holiday, leisure and time off. We believe it is a fantastic way to take your life to the next level. To use your long term trip to really do what you're dreaming about, as the starting point of your new life, as a way of taking yourself to a place you'd never imagine yourself being before you set off (both physically and mentally).
- What stops most people from really going on that dream journey? What's stopping you?
- How do people take themselves past all the different obstacles that inevitably stand in the way when they make a decision to go away for an extended time? How can it be possible for you to take yourself past the different obstacles that stand in your way?
- How do you want to travel? How can you create the perfect trip that suites you and the circumstances you are in?

So our intention is to make it clear to you both *that* it is, and *how* it is, possible for you too to make a longer journey. What we want to provide you with, is a book that gives you the insights and the confidence to get to the point where you're ready to go out and buy that guidebook on Australia or reserve your flight ticket to Kuala Lumpur or rent an apartment in Barcelona or whatever next step you'll feel encouraged to do. Hope we'll succeed!

3. A Little Bit About Us

We, who believe that you can quit your job and take the kids out of school and travel the world – that Extended World Travel is totally a possibility for you too, are a Swedish family of five. Thanks to some choices we made and the traveling we've done, we have created a situation where we very much are living our dream life. For many years we have been living a life that has allowed us to study and work from wherever we went. We've experienced loads of interesting and exciting things together. We have friends all over the world and we very much feel and see ourselves not only as Swedes, but as World Citizens.

Now this is us, but don't limit yourself by thinking that being exactly like we are is the only way to do some long term travel. On our journeys, we have met people from all walks of life and in all kinds of circumstances, traveling around the globe.

We have met single parents traveling with their children, as well as families with five children. We've connected with people who travel even though they are in a wheelchair or over the age of ninety. We've connected directly with people in all kinds of circumstances who travel extensively and we want you to know that it is a possibility for you too, no matter where you are in life.

We do not claim that the way we have traveled is the only way either. A claim like that would be a bit arrogant, (being Swedes and all…). And remember that the knowledge we are sharing in this book, is based not only on our own experience, but also on the experiences of hundreds of other passionate travelers.

"I haven't been everywhere, but it's on my list."
- Susan Sontag

As for our own world travel journey, we (the parents) started our traveling adventures very early in our lives. Our parents gave us this gift by taking us to beautiful and unusual places long before world travel became main stream, and we've never stopped.

Our aim has never been to visit as many different countries as possible, and there are many travelers out there who have seen way more places then we have. Places we have been so far include Norway, Finland, Denmark, Holland, Austria, Belgium, Germany, Switzerland, Italy, France, Spain, Poland, Rumania, Greece, England, Canary Islands, Morocco, Tunisia, Israel, Thailand, USA, (10 states), Canada, Fiji, New Zealand, Australia, India, Sri Lanka. Many of these places we visited over and over again, and some we lived in for long periods. And that's really what we are passionate about and want to share with Extended World Travel; how to travel long term. During the last fifteen year period we have made seven longer trips - around six months, and of course, lots of shorter ones as well.

So we guess we can say that traveling is natural for us; it's simply how we think.

We went on our first extended journey as a family in the mid 90's. It was a five month trip through Europe in a campervan. It is one of the most amazing experiences we've ever had and it impacted us all and changed our lives forever. It made us realize what's really important to us. We became more harmonious and happy and it also helped us to get out of the 9 to 5 — which we never returned to. So our first long term journey got us hooked, and there really was no going back. After that, we very much created a whole life style that made it possible to live in ways that suited us best and that gave room for being able to travel and to live for longer periods wherever we wanted.

So, as a family, we have literary spent years traveling and living abroad, experiencing many different parts of our wonderful world and connecting with all kinds of fantastic people.

One of the incredible things we've discovered is that when you travel for extended periods of time, you experience all kinds of mental clarity. Simply by getting away from your everyday struggle in the Rat Race, your views on life naturally begin to change. You get new perspective on what's really important to you

The experience of long term travel is so powerful and one of the main reasons why we wanted to create our blog as well as this book. To show you that this opportunity is available for you too! We wish that more people would take the chance to feel more alive and discover their ideal way of living.

We truly believe from the depth of our hearts that Extended World Traveling is GOOD for you! Not only good for you, but it will also profoundly benefit the people around you and as an extension, the whole world!

We are committed to helping you take your travel dreams seriously and really go for it. And we're looking forward to one day meet you in person somewhere in the world.

Happy Travels!

4. Why Do You Want to Travel the World?

"It was a day like this when Marco Polo took off to China. What are your plans today?"
- Loesje

Today, most people live in ways which are, to a very big extent, planned. When the alarm goes off in the morning, you know pretty well what will happen throughout the day. You'll have your breakfast (we assume most of you who read this don't have to worry if there's going to be any breakfast), go off to work and send the kids to school...You also have a pretty good idea of what the day at work, or school, will look like. Then you head back home where you might have some planned activities, maybe TV or a movie, or some time in front of the computer, and off you go to bed. You get up the next day and run the program over again, and again, and again...

Don't get us wrong here, we do believe it's important to remember to be grateful. Grateful for having things like a safe home, food on the table, and an income as well as good health and people who love and appreciate us.

Nevertheless, to many, there's still something missing. In the midst of your well known, successful and abundant life, a feeling of emptiness sometimes pops up. Or feelings of boredom, restlessness, unhappiness or maybe of not being fully alive. What's often missing in your well planned perfectly scheduled life, is a touch of the unknown and the unplanned - of excitement and adventure!

Aurora takes an audio guided tour at Stonehenge

Spring in the Netherlands. Aurora in one of the huge tulip fields.

Olive harvest at Arenalejos, Southern Spain. Best oil ever!

Our first mobile home. It took us to Spain and back to Sweden!

People say that what we are seeking is a meaning for life. I don't think this is what we're really seeking. I think what we're seeking is an experience of being alive"
- Joseph Campbell

What we've more and more subtracted from our lives today, are opportunities to experience the unknown, situations where we neither know what to expect nor how to act. Situations where you really have to access all of your capabilities, assemble your strengths and creativity, and see what you really go for. That's when you really feel like you are living and that's part of why we, and so many others, love to travel.

"On one hand, we hunger for new challenges that will test our resolve, on the other, we feel perfectly miserable when subjected to the usual hardship that accompany adventures. These ambivalent feelings are, in fact, the best indicators that we are smack in the middle of an adventure. It is when you say to yourself, as Thornton Wilder did in The Matchmaker 'Oh, now I've got myself into an awful mess; I wish I were sitting quietly at home'. Of course, Wilder continues, you know you are really in trouble 'when you sit quietly at home wishing you were out having lots of adventures'".
- Jeffrey Kottler, from the book "Travel that will change your life"

When we discuss "WHY TRAVEL?" (and by that we mean "why go on a long journey?") with people, the answer can seem obvious at first: to have fun, to relax, to find adventure. But when you think about it some more, there are so many other different reasons behind these. We're all motivated by our different circumstances and needs so the answers to this are really as many as there are people

Some travel to leave something, like a boring job, a relationship or a family situation that doesn't work or just old habits. Others are more motivated by going towards something. Their answer to "why travel" is more about seeking adventure, meeting new people, seeing new things, creating a new relationship to one or more fellow travelers (or to themselves).

Usually though, it's a combination of both. We travel because we want to leave something behind and at the same time, we want to experience all this new. This is really a perfect combination, because when we both let go of the old stuff and create an environment where new things can enter, we really have the opportunity to take our lives to a totally different level.

The reasons for traveling vary for everybody; we all have our personal story that drives us to want to go out in the world. In addition we have come up with some reasons which we think are important to consider when you're thinking about this. So, check them out and see which ones resonate with you, and then allow yourself to take them seriously!

Because You Want To

To acknowledge and take action on your desires is important so this reason is as good as any. Whether you're dreaming about long term travel or something else, pursuing your dreams inspires you and makes you happy. It also makes you a stronger person and gives you control in your life.

Just think for a minute about the alternative, not following your dream. Imagine something or someone stopping you from doing what you really want. Doesn't feel very good, does it?

If you don't reach for your dream of traveling you are giving up a lot more than a journey. You are giving up experience and adventure but more than that, you are giving up parts of yourself. You are settling for something less than you want, deserve and are capable of.

Following your dreams validates you as a person and underlines what is important to you. Sure, we know we are talking about long term travel, but for many people travel is a life-long dream.

Furthermore, if you're more happy and satisfied, you can do more good in the world than if you're stressed and depressed. So don't ask yourself who you are to take your desires seriously but rather, who are you not to?

I prefer to be a dreamer among the humblest, with visions to be realized, than lord among those without dreams and desires.
- Kahlil Gibran

To Experience the World

One of the primary reasons for travel is to discover more of the world you live in. Another reason is escape – to escape the world you live in and go somewhere else for a while.

There are so many fantastic places to see, both well known ones as well as places you've never heard of (which often tend to be the most interesting). And wherever you go and whatever you do, you'll be sure to get some perspective on your own life and your own way of doing things. It's always refreshing to see things from a different angle and to learn that your own way is not the only, or necessarily the best way. And even though it is good to see different places and sites, the real benefits from traveling are usually the meetings with new people. That's what helps you open your mind and learn more, both about different cultures as well as yourself.

"We live in a wonderful world that is full of beauty, charm and adventure. There is no end to the adventures we can have if only we seek them with our eyes open."
– Jawaharial Nehru

It is possible to discover the world a little piece at a time by talking shorter trips. In fact, you may even get to see more of it this way – but you won't experience it in quite the same way as when you travel for a longer time. As a long term traveler you are usually not in the same hurry as someone who's just on a short vacation. For us traveling is not about collecting sites, cities, or countries but more about experiencing life in different places. We have chosen to go to fewer destinations but stayed for a longer period of time in each of them. We wanted to find out what it's like to live in different places, get to know the people and their customs. And it's always refreshing to get some of your prejudice crushed. You may think that your way of doing things is the only way for example (little do you know) and then when you go around the world, you see that there are so many different ways to live and to do things. And some of these ways and ideas hit home with you, so you bring them back and incorporate them into your own life, and you then get the best of two worlds, or rather, of many worlds.

And also, don't forget that the world is constantly changing and the things you might be interested in experiencing may not be there any more if you wait too long. Like Magnus for example who, all his youth, had a wish to see the Berlin Wall in person. One day the opportunity vanished. We were lucky enough though to get to the top of the World Trade Center before the opportunity vanished.

To Take a Break from Life's Routine and to Recharge Your Batteries

As a consequence of traveling for extended periods and of being able to let go of so many stressful things back home, we've created the freedom to discover what we really want in life. Although traveling can have its challenges at times, we've realized it can be so much more stressful to us in our home environment where there are always lots of things calling for attention as well as a perennial lack of time. But since we set things up to go away for a longer period of time we've been able to live more in the moment and our stress level has decreased.

When you let go of the things that constantly draw your attention and have time to think about other aspects of your life, interesting things start to happen. For us, we stopped making the same old choices automatically. Being in new circumstances, we were faced with new challenges and suddenly, without realizing it, we were asking ourselves not what we *had* to do but what we *wanted* to do. This change of perception may not sound like much but it has had a major influence on our life. Every time we get back after a long journey, we've made some major change. We've cleared out old stuff and ideas that no longer serve us and only kept the things we still want in our lives.

No matter what you do in life and how much you like it, sooner or later it becomes routine. There is nothing wrong with that, except that over time routine becomes less amusing and turns into what you *have* to do rather than what you *want* to do. And when you're too much caught up in all the "have to's" and somewhere inside you feel that there's something else you want but you can't really get access to it, a long journey is a fantastic way to let go and get your priorities right.

"Travel and change of place impart new vigor to the mind."
– *Seneca*

A one or two week vacation will give you a break and help you to get superficially relaxed, but it won't really give you time to recharge your batteries, experience some deeper relaxation and get a fresh perspective. A short break simply doesn't allow you enough time to de-stress and to reflect upon whether your routine is something which brings joy to your life or if it's just something that has turned in to a bad habit.

But before you go off on a long journey you have to prepare for it and make decisions about what you are going to do with all the different

21

aspects of your life. You will need to make some preparation so that you really can let go of everything when you're away. Things like whether you will close up your home, rent it out or even sell it? Store your car or get rid of it? Request leave from work or create more freedom for yourself by just resigning? And you will have to look into what you will you do with your mail and who will take care of the bills.

Once this is done though, once you have sorted out your old life, you don't have to worry about it for the duration of the journey. And this will create tons of freedom for you! The things that usually take all of your attention when you are at home will be taken care of and you can spend your time taking things as they come and just be. And this will really help you to unwind and get reenergized and to see what's really important to you and give you an opportunity to set your priorities right. How cool is that?

To Improve All Your Relationships

There is a common belief among those who haven't tried it yet, that your marriage or the relationship with your kids wouldn't survive if you spent loads of time together on a long trip. This is not our experience at all and neither the experience of almost all the travelers we have met throughout the years. On the contrary, the vast majority of them say that their relationships have greatly improved. Those who don't, usually agree that their relationship wouldn't have survived even if they had stayed at home.

There isn't much time to look after our relationships in our everyday lives. There are couples who hardly get the chance to see each other because of their working hours and other commitments, and there are parents and children who only meet in the early morning or late at night when they all are exhausted or stressed out. Living under these circumstances doesn't allow much room for enjoying and improving relationships and making them stronger.

One of the biggest advantages of traveling together for an extended period is that you can reconnect with people close to you and rediscover who they are. You can have fun together and learn new things about yourselves and about the world.

This is especially true for kids. Kids are the sunshine in our lives, but way too often we almost feel like they are a burden. This is so sad and if this is your experience, we really recommend that you do some extensive traveling together. Spending more time with your children is a good thing. The concept of small amounts of "quality time" doesn't always work. Have you ever experienced having planned some really fun quality time like Christmas or Disneyland and it turns into a disaster? Expectations can be so high at occasions like this that there is no way to live up to them.

To go away on a long journey gives you lots of time together. You get the good as well as the bad (whatever that is) and from the quantity time, quality times will emerge. The times we have spent traveling with each other and our children have almost exclusively been an absolute joy for us. They have brought us closer together and we now share lots of great memories. So for us, traveling has really improved our relationship and helped us to grow closer to each others.

"I have found out that there ain't no surer way to find out whether you like people or hate them than to travel with them."
– Mark Twain

Before It's too Late

This is really critical for everyone between the ages of twenty five and sixty five. There is a well-accepted myth that if you want to go on a long journey you have to do it when you're under twenty five, preferably single and have no commitments and are still "free." Otherwise you will have to wait until you reach retirement age and freedom once more comes your way.

This is just too terrible to even think about. How can it be that so many give up their freedom only to reclaim it forty years later? During these forty years you are in the prime of your life and want to see, explore, educate yourself, feel free and live as well!

Why not choose freedom now? Even if you have a family and kids, a home and a steady job there are still lots of possibilities to travel the world. All we are saying is that if you have a dream, do something about it before it is too late! Don't let obligations and the expectations of others suck the joy out of your life.

It's way too common for people that we meet to say "I dream of traveling but I will have to do it later." Then they reel off a whole list of reasons for not doing it now. Usually the reasons go something like this:

- I don't have the money
- I don't have the time
- My children are too young
- My children are too old
- I have a home to take care of
- My work or business prevents me from going away

We call these reasons the BUTs. And if you are letting the Buts stop you now you run a big risk of letting the same Buts or other new ones stop you later on too.

On the other hand if you do turn your dream into reality later on (which is really great of course) it won't be the same as doing it now. We have met and seen many who finally get to live their dream life - at the age of seventy... many of them wishing they had done something earlier. Realizing that the things they were dreaming of at the age of thirty, forty or fifty no longer are the things they want to do at seventy - it's suddenly too late for them.

Don't let yourself get trapped by the "I'll do it later syndrome." If you have a dream, start taking action towards it **now!** Who knows what will happen in the future? If you wait too long it might just be too late, and you don't want that to happen do you?

"All those days that came and went, I didn't know that was life"
- Stig Johansson, Swedish Poet

Because You Won't Regret It

Chances are that if you don't do it now, you will regret it later on. It is easy to think you will do something tomorrow, next month, next year or even in ten years time. But when time passes and you still haven't done it, there is no way to get your life back to do it over. There is nothing you can do to change your past. It is the choices you make now, today, that decide what your future past will look like.

We heard a priest many years ago talking about the many elderly people he had visited and talked to. And he said almost all of them shared one thing: they expressed that there was nothing they regretted having done. What they did regret though, was the things they really had wanted to do, but never did!

Do you honestly think that you will ever regret:

- The time you take off from work to make your dream a reality?
- The extra time you spend with your loved ones?
- The fact that you respected your heart's desire and realized your dream?

So far we have never met anyone who regrets their decision to go on an extended journey. Sometimes it hasn't turned out exactly as they imagined. But regrets? NO WAY!

Most of them bless the day they made their decision and took action to go.

Who do you choose to believe? Those who have the actual experience or the little voice in your head that creates all the Buts? Or your family, friends, colleagues or neighbors, who have never done anything like a long voyage themselves, and who are happily encouraging your BUTs by expressing their own fear?

Sure, staying at home is probably the safe and sensible choice to make. At least, that's what many seem to say. But the question is, will it set your spirit on fire? Will it make your heart beat faster? Will it inspire you? Will it make you feel fully alive?

For some, staying at home may be the thrill of their life. But our guess is that if you are reading this you are not one of them. And if you aren't, then you better do something about it or you run the risk of regretting it later.

"The alternative is looking ahead twenty years and, not having heeded your heart, seeing yourself devoted to the wrong job, married to the wrong partner, saying 'I wish I would have at least tried when I had the chance.' And for me, that's just too risky."
- Kelly from "Kelly's gone again"

To Know Your Why Helps You Solve Your How

Going on a long journey is something a lot of people dream of and talk about and we all have different reasons for wishing to do so. So what's your reason?

Why should you take time to think about this, isn't it enough that you just want to go away you may wonder? Of course if you have a strong enough desire, you just fix whatever need to be done and leave, but oftentimes, it's just not that easy and you might need some help to take action and to get everything into place. Being clear about why you want to travel actually helps you to attract all kinds of possibilities and solutions that will make it a lot easier to make your trip a reality.

It is said that by knowing the why, you will be 80% on the way to make things happen! What to do and how to do it, is then only the remaining 20%!

So the more clear you are about your why and the stronger you feel about why you want something the easier it is for the how's to happen!

We encourage you to think about it for a while. And in the meantime check out what some experienced travelers we've talked to have to say about this.

First out is our friend Litsong from Taiwan. Litsong, is a real globetrotter who travels the world regularly and for extended time periods, mostly with her son. When we asked her why she travels, she said this, which we think really sums it up in a great way:

"I travel so I can have a change of pace and path in my life. Traveling helps me to still my curiosity about people, to create new possibilities for my livelihood and to discover new places. It gives me the opportunity to be with friends, both new and old and the opportunity to live in the present, being in the here and now and having fun!"

Denice from NotAnotherTourist.com expresses it like this.:

"One of the greatest things about traveling is that you get to become like a child again. You are totally helpless in a new place and have to observe and learn as you go. You have the unique opportunity to wrap your head around new ways to do everything from using the bathroom to getting along in a group. So the biggest advantage of being a traveler is opening your mind to a whole new way of thinking and living. When you start to see the parameters and roles that are defined for people in other cultures, you begin to see similar or opposite parameters defined in your own culture. You begin to realize there is no 'us' versus 'them' and that everyone has a different way of doing things. In essence, the further you go away from home, the closer you get to finding out who you are."

Derek from Oneyearonearth.com says:

"Travel gives you perspective and enrichment. For those who haven't seen the diversity in the world (whether race, culture, religion, food, political beliefs or income levels), it's virtually impossible to understand your place in the world. Only travel provides this."

Finally we want to share some thought about this from Wade from Vagabondjourney.com:

"Travel changes, makes, and builds you as a person, and once the ball is in motion it becomes difficult to stop. As Chatwin once wrote, 'Travel does not merely broaden the mind, it makes the mind . . .' Traveling is a process of building the self. The external landscapes through which you roam is just the kaleidoscopic backdrop to the real action — the real action is the changes in perception and first hand knowledge that happens within you as you travel. It does not matter an ounce if I am in the jungles of Amazonia or riding a bike in Portugal or working on an archaeology project in Arizona, the travel process — the internal process of blending observation, impression, and experience, figuring out yourself and the world you live in — is the same. The place is merely the background, the map is merely the impetus for finding those empty moments for pondering which can really make a life tick...

It is my impression that traveling is not only an action that takes you farther, but also further, deeper. Deeper into yourself, perhaps, further into building the blocks of a life well spent: a life of memories, learning, understanding. A life of decoding the riddles of what makes you happy — this is the prime directive of travel.

It is my impression that this is the benefit of traveling"

To give some focus to the question, "Why Travel?" is foundational if you are planning to turn your travel dreams into reality. So, please take some time to think about this now!

- Why do you want to go on an extended trip?
- What specifically motivates you to do some long term traveling?
- What do you want to experience?
- What do you see your trip leading to?
- Who do you want to be when you get back?
- What is your biggest motivation to travel?

Think about this and get yourself a really strong Why!

5. What's Stopping You From Going on That Long Trip of Your Dreams – What Are Your BUTs?

"It is not because things are difficult that we do not dare; it is because we do not dare that they are difficult."
- Seneca

You'd Love To Travel, BUT...

When we are traveling or when we talk to people about long term travel they almost never ask us about our journeys and our adventures or how to actually travel. Instead, the most common question is: "What do you do for a living?" But we've come to realized that people are not really interested in our jobs or what we actually do for a living. What they really want to find out is how they themselves can get the time, the money and the possibility to travel and live a life like we do.

When we start to tell about the choices we've made regarding time, money, work, school and other aspects of our life, it's very common to hear people say something like:

"Well, I'd love to travel and live like that too, BUT..."

And then they start to explain and give us reasons to why it just isn't a possibility for them and why they can't do it.

In the pool in Fiji, reading about Australia Zoo before going there

Aron playing on the beach (all the time) on Nacula Island, Fiji

Finally, arriving at the "real" Hobbiton, in Matamata, New Zealand!

Ready to swim with dolphins, in Akaroa, New Zealand

"The reason your dreams get obstructed, is because, 'cleaning your closets' or 'making phone calls' – are given more value in that immediate moment than your dreams"
- Blair Singer

We've realized, that when we (yes, we too) start dreaming about something we want to do, all kinds of roadblocks, Buts, as we call them, seem to turn up placing themselves between us and the dreams we are yearning for.

What are your BUTs? Most often what we hear after "I'd love to travel, BUT" is usually something like:

- I don't have the money
- I don't have the time
- I have my job and my career to think about
- My children have to go to school
- My family wouldn't approve and my friends would think I'm crazy
- I'm terrified of flying
- I'm to scared of catching some exotic disease
- I'm really worried about crime and violence or becoming a victim of terrorism

We all have our different road blocks or things we experience as obstacles which pops up in our minds when we start thinking about doing, or making a decision to do something new with our life. Regarding traveling, and especially long term travel and being away for months or even years, there are lots of different fears that can challenge us and prevent us from taking the roads we want to travel.

This is not to say that there's anything wrong with having these concerns, or that they are not real. The question is how much you'll let them stop you?

Furthermore, we're all, to a larger or lesser extent, caught up with our everyday issues and concerns which prevent us from dreaming about what we really want, let alone truly going after it.

For many people, just thinking about what we have to organize to do some extended traveling, makes us feel exhausted and overwhelmed.

But there's always a solution to everything and there are always ways to get past your roadblocks. Truly there are! And the more you are willing and inspired to arrive at that specific destination, the more ways you'll find and the easier it will be to pass what's blocking your way. Or rather, what you might perceive as blocking your way.

Actually, there are people from all walks of life (yes, we really mean ALL walks of life) who DO travel the world. For as many people who allow their Buts to stand in their way, there are also people who rise above them and go after their dreams!

All Kinds of Travelers

On our own journeys, we have met travelers with all kinds of occupations and backgrounds: nurses, teachers, plumbers, doctors, janitors, lawyers, taxi drivers, and shop assistants, to name a few.

We've met traveling families with babies, young children and with older teenagers. We've connected with single mothers, single fathers as well as families with five children. We've met unemployed travelers, travelers in wheelchairs and even travelers who've celebrated their ninetieth birthday.

Being a traveler is not really about your income level, your age or family situation.

Being a traveler is more about acknowledging your dreams and allowing yourself to follow them.

If all these people we've met can do it, we promise you that you can too!

Of course, we all have our obstacles, our "yeah-buts" to overcome on our path to our dream destinations. But if you are deeply committed to going on a long term journey we promise you that there are always ways to get there - always!

Find Your BUT...

"There's fear that keeps you alive. And there's fear that keeps you from living. Wisdom is knowing the difference."
- David Swenson

We encourage you to take a few moments and look deeper at your roadblocks. What are the specific challenges that keep you at home in your old circumstances instead of out there, traveling the world and fulfilling your dreams?

Imagine your spouse, your child or friend coming up to you and suggesting; "why don't we just go away for some time, travel, leave all this and explore the world"? What's the first thing that comes up in your mind (and the second, third)?

What are you afraid could happen if you just left and went on that dream trip? Or what would happen when you get back? Or perhaps during the trip itself? Or maybe even before? Will you catch a disease? Go bankrupt? Lose your friends? Or maybe your kids will fall behind in school?

What is that little voice in your head saying that tells you it's too difficult, or not even possible?

Notice what it says and see if it fits into any of the categories that we talk about on the following pages. If it does, you might get some hints or ideas about what you can do to overcome your strongest buts and start to take the steps necessary for creating your long dream journey.

"I am willing to say to anybody that the only thing that stands between me and what I want is between my right ear and my left ear"
- Blair Singer

You'd love to travel the world, but you just don't have the money

It's the absolute most common remark we get when we talk to people about our travels. In a way, it's probably often true. But seen in another perspective, many times it's probably not.

When we look at our financial lives, it often consists of things like mortgages, food, clothing, insurance, cars, bills, schools, entertainment, and other expenses. With all this, how could it be possible for you to have the money for an extended trip around the world? Where will your money come from? You barely have enough for your everyday expenses, how on earth would you be able to take an expensive, exclusive trip around the world – maybe with your whole family?

And of course, it's true that you do need money to travel, but usually not at all as much as you might think.

The fact is that those who do travel the world are almost never people who suddenly find themselves with an abundance of money they don't know what to do with (except for a few lottery winners and such). Nor are they people with an especially high income or rich parents.

People who travel the world are, in terms of income, very much like everybody else!

The difference between a world traveler and the ones who remain at home is that as a world traveler you:

- Acknowledge that you have this dream of going on a journey.
- Nurture this travel dream and keep it alive.
- Take inspired action in the direction of your dream.

So, to keep the dream alive and growing is what will become the creative generator for creating the money you'll need for your travels.

"A journey of a thousand miles begins with a cash advance."
- Bumper sticker

Regarding money for traveling, there are questions you need to ask yourself when you're planning for an extended world trip, like:

- How much money do I need for my trip, what will it actually cost?
- How much do I have already?
- If I don't have enough for what I want to do, how can I raise more?

At first it can be overwhelming to even think about all this. However, we can cover some basics by dividing up the topic into two parts, namely generating money and changing your lifestyle:

Generating Money to Travel:

You won't necessarily have to actually generate all the money you need for your trip with your present working income. You can also generate money if you:

A. Look at what you really have already
B. Change your lifestyle
C. Work as you go
D. Find new sources of income

A. Look at what you already have

There are many things to consider and implement to get access to, or free money that you already have, including opening your mind to some new ways of thinking.

As Albert Einstein said:

"We can't solve problems by using the same kind of thinking we used when we created them."

What do you own that you could live without?

Maybe you have things you could sell to raise cash for some life-changing travel opportunities? Traveling can become the foundation for a journey that will take you to the next level in your life. Perhaps there are some possessions you own that connect you to a life that doesn't fulfill you anymore?

Look for things that tie you to a way of living that isn't working for you. It could be your house, your apartment, your car (or several cars?) Perhaps you have accumulated lots of "stuff" over the years. Look for things that sap your time and energy in maintenance. Instead of wasting time and money taking care of these things you could sell them and make someone else happy as well as raising money to make yourself happy!

If it's a too drastic step sell your home, consider renting it out. This will generate money to cover your mortgage while you are off exploring the world. Make a list of things you own and check off the things that you could live without.

Consider selling them, renting them out or exchanging them for something else you need and would otherwise have to purchase. Think of ways to make better use of your possessions in creative ways rather than just owning them.

As someone said to us the other day "If your house burned down to the ground and everything else with it, what would you buy again"? Hmm, interesting thought…

B. Change Your Lifestyle

How much is your lifestyle costing you?

What are you paying for your home, home maintenance, your mortgage, your car(s) your credit card payments?

What does your job actually cost you? Include things like the special clothes you buy for work, commuting costs (we talked to a neighbor the other day who told us he spends 10% of his salary in commuting costs alone), lunches out, the fancy Café Latte on the way to work that you would not otherwise buy – not to mention the after work activities you need to relax after all the hard work you've been putting in.

Think about what you spend on kids' activities, toys, etc.

Often you think you don't have the money but if you take the time to sit down and figure out what you are actually spending in "necessities" you could be in for a surprise.

Rearranging your lifestyle can take you a very long way towards realizing a traveling dream. Maybe you already have what it takes if you just change your priorities a bit. Or maybe you can just make some small adjustments and be ready to go a lot earlier than you first imagined.

C. Work As You Go

To work while you travel is an option if you want to earn extra money along the way or stay longer than your budget allows. For some people, it is possible to bring their work with them and then just continue with the normal tasks but in new and different locations.

An American friend of ours traveled the world for many years with his computer, continuing to work for his company from different places around the world. He used to send us pictures from his "office view" of the day. A sunny beach in the Caribbean, a busy city in Europe, a tropical forest in Asia (and, of course, he didn't work all the time).

The kind of work that is easiest to find along the way is seasonal work like fruit picking, jobs in tourist areas (ski resorts, restaurants, cruises) and if English is your native language, teaching English is an option in a lot places in the world.

Some friends of ours, a family of five, spent a winter doing different seasonal jobs in Southern Europe. First they caught the grape harvesting season in Southern France, where they all participated (according to their abilities) in picking grapes. They then continued a bit further south to Spain and The Pyrenees, and stayed at a resort where the mother offered massages and the father, who's an avid cook, helped out in the kitchen. Then, being Swedish and used to snow and skiing, the whole family worked as ski teachers, helping people who were unaccustomed to the mountains in wintertime.

Another English friend of ours found a job on a cruise ship and spent a year cruising around the world doing different jobs on ships.

Of course, today there are also great possibilities to create an income from the internet which allows you to work from anywhere. You can both look for "regular" jobs which are done over the internet or create your own business.

Travel writing, affiliate marketing, having a special theme for your trip and getting sponsors for it are some options.

So if you're a bit creative in your thinking, there are many options to work while you travel. If you really want some inspiration and great information about travel and work, have a look at this site: www.transitionsabroad.com

D. Find New Sources of Income

To generate money from new sources usually involves getting an extra job or putting more hours into the one you already have. In both cases, it's important to be disciplined to really save this money for the trip. Putting it in a special travel account and just keeping it there is crucial!

Adjusting Your Travel Plan

If it is important for you to only stay in 5 star hotels and eat in restaurants when you're out in the world, it goes without saying that you need a bigger travel budget than if you are focusing on Network Traveling and mainly staying for free. Maybe you want a bit of both?

Do you want to travel mainly in countries in the Western world or are you interested in exploring other cultures? Are you open to travel in cultures where the standard of living may not be what you are used to - nor the cost of living?

Consider this: if you have a house or apartment in some western country and rent it out while you travel, a month's rent from your house could actually help you pay for a cottage on a paradise beach in, for example, South East Asia for half a year! Or what you pay for a single evening out at your favorite fancy restaurant could feed you for a couple of weeks in a low cost country. Someone mentioned that for the amount of money that it costs to fill up your car, you can take the train across the whole of China! Think about that next time you are standing there at the gas station!

Then, of course, there is the possibility to exchange your home with people in some other part of the world where you would like to go. You still have your fixed costs but you'll be staying for free. More about this in "How to travel."

Worth noticing also is that it's a lot less expensive to travel for the longer term than doing several short trips. It's usually transportation that eats up the most money. Also, when you travel for several months (or even years) you usually don't spend every day going on costly sightseeing tours, eating at restaurants, spending that "little extra because it's your vacation…"

You find other ways of traveling and living. You often become a bit more like a local and your days are more about "everyday living in a new environment." You learn things like where the locals do their shopping (not in the tourist areas). And also the fact that you have more time; time to choose cheaper ways of doing things, like finding less costly, quality staple foods for preparing your meals rather than having to settle for expensive readymade food or restaurants. Or just spend days doing things that are free, like reading, walking, talking to people - just because you have the time.

A busy life encourages us to live in ways that use more money. In fact, extended travel can even be much cheaper than staying at home! Rolf Potts, famous world traveler, says in his book "Vagabonding" that travel does not really cost that much, maintaining things does!

A Norwegian family we met in Fiji had just sold their house to do something else for a whole year rather than just living in it.

"Soultravelers3," an American family of three, also sold their home in California to be able to have a free traveling lifestyle. They have now been traveling the world, mostly Europe, since 2006, and have also created extra income by writing about their way of living. They also agree that being on the road can be a lot cheaper than staying at home.

An American friend rearranged his job to be able to take it with him and work a couple of hours a day from anywhere in the world.

Someone else, who really understood that a world trip would be an investment in herself, took out a loan.

Also, a very common way to create money to travel is to just get rid of certain expenses and take an extra job for a while.

You can focus on one of these, but putting your attention on all of them will of course speed up the process.

Acknowledge your dream to travel, commit to it, address the money issue and you will soon be on your way!

"Rich people play the money game to win. Poor people play the money game to not lose."
- T Harv Eker

You'd Love to Travel but You Don't Have the Time

What's your first thought when someone mentions extended traveling? Do you ask yourself; "How on earth would I get the time to go on a six month trip when my life is so busy already?" Or "With everything

I'm involved in, how would I ever get the time to do some long term traveling?" Or maybe "Well, long term travel, that's really for people without a job or a family and other obligations that take up all of your time." Or maybe even "In my life, there will certainly not be any time for real travel until I'm retired!" And if you are like most people, your day is probably filled with things like work, overtime work, commuting, studies, children, school, home work, shopping, cooking, driving, activities, hobbies, telephone calls, e-mails, TV, to name just a few. So sure, how would you be able to cram a six, nine or even just a three month journey into your busy life? Where would you find the time?

You Create the Time

We'll tell you a secret. You don't get the time. You never will. You claim the time! People who travel the world for extended periods are usually not people who suddenly find themselves with a bunch of extra time that they don't know how to fill. The vast majority of travelers are people just like you, with schedules filled to the brim. And one day, they get this idea. This idea about something else... something more - a different life! They allow this idea to be there and they put their focus on it. They nourish it and help it grow. And that makes all the difference!

"Vagabonding is about refusing to exile travel to some other seemingly appropriate time of your life."
- Rolf Potts

When we took the time...

At one stage in our lives, everything became just too much. Our own company consumed all our time. Whatever was (wasn't) left of the time, we used for driving the children to school and other places, cleaning and refurbishing our huge old house and all the other everyday activities.

Then one day, we reached the limit and felt we'd just had enough. We realized we wanted more out of life and started to dream about something else. We were longing for time to just be together as a family and experience the world. We wanted excitement and adventure as well as a slower pace and time for each other. We wanted time to travel! We wrote a letter (this was before the days of e-mail) to the traveling section of one of the nation's biggest newspapers:

"How do we take our family to New Zealand (the other side of the world to us) and find ways to create money when we travel around there?"

They published our question together with some very inspiring answers. Wow, we had started a ball rolling! The travel idea now really had planted itself in our minds. We had taken the first step and we were practically on our way! No, we didn't go to NZ this time though (but we did later). We bought an old campervan instead and went through Europe to Southern Spain for five months. And even if it wasn't as exotic to us as NZ, it was the best use we had ever made of our time. To leave all the time consuming activities that we were caught up in at home and just BE! We suddenly had the time to really listen and talk to each other, the time to think a thought to the end.

This abundance of time helped us to gain a perspective on our lives and to see what was really important to us. What did we want to keep of the things we used to do and what did we not want when we returned? This trip turned out to be the beginning of a totally new life for us.

Now, looking back, this was one of the best and one of the most life changing decisions we have made. It led us on totally new roads, both literally and mentally. It was everything we had imagined and much more. We came back after half a year as rather different people. More relaxed, more inspired, closer to each other, and full of ideas on how we could live our lives in a different way. We didn't join the Rat Race again and we haven't been there since.

Today, we're very glad that we prioritized to take the time and really went on that first long term trip of ours. Many more have followed but this first was the one that really got us on the "live the life you choose" track.

"Time is free, but it's priceless. You can't own it, but you can use it. You can't keep it, but you can spend it. Once you've lost it you can never get it back."
- Loesje

Time is Life...

Time is life and time is your most important resource. Do you use it as such? When talking about time, it's good to start to think about what you want to get out of your life. In our lives today, we have a multitude of directions to go. There are so many things we can do (not to mention all the things we think we "must" and "should" do). We have access to an infinite mass of information. We know (at least in theory) that everything is possible… If we're not aware of what's important to us, what we really want to give our time/life to, it's extremely easy to get overwhelmed, and even burned out. In these times of abundant choices, now, more than ever, it's essential to find out and decide which way you want to go and what you want to put your focus on.

We often hear people say things like "In my life, there's no time to travel". By the way how often do you yourself use the expression "I don't have the time"? For a lot of people, usually several times a day. But, how can you actually say that? Of course you have the time! What you really should be saying is something more like, "I don't want to take the time for this" or even "I choose not to prioritize this"! Different, isn't it.

For people today, especially in the "western world", you're aware that there are so many ways you can choose to live your life. You know that "the possibilities are endless" as well as the fact that "you create your life." So what will you choose to be and do and have? It's easy to get frustrated over all the alternatives that exist that you can give your precious time to. Should you really make room for some time to travel?

If you take a look at your life right now and what you've filled it with, do you remember why you chose the things you did? Was it because you were totally passionate about these things? Or because someone else thought this is what you should be using some of your life for? Or, are you using your time to do whatever you're doing at the moment, so you can do something else that'll make you happy later, in the future? If that's the case, why not be happy now as well? Time is on your side!

You are given this amount of time, 24 hours every day. What do you want to do with it (yes, more choices)? What do you want to use the next 8760 hours (one year) for? Or the next six months? Or next month? Next week? Tomorrow?

When you start to look into how you really would want to use your precious time, it's a bit like moving into a totally new home. Imagine that you have this empty new place that you're just about to move in to. You can furnish it exactly the way you want. So what do you really want it to look like? Which of all your old stuff do you want to put in here? All of it? Maybe you want to get some new things? Or do you want to get rid of all the old ones and have everything brand new? Or maybe mix old and new? In that case, which parts of the old stuff do you want to keep? Maybe you even want to move into a totally empty place and then see, along the way, what will suit you best to fill it with?

It 's the same thing with your time. Do an inventory of your time; what are you filling it up with at the moment? Take a look in your calendar. When you look at all the "stuff" that fills up your days, your weeks, your years, what would you really want to keep? What excites you? What makes you feel depressed? What would you like to exchange for something different? What makes you get in touch with that feeling of passion?

If you had an empty house, or rather, an empty calendar, and had the possibility to fill it with whatever you want, what would that be? Which things would you want to prioritize to put there in your brand new time schedule (some time to travel maybe)? What would reflect the person you are today and give your life more meaning and support you to become a happier person?

So, go get a new calendar and start fantasizing!

Also, if you do want to travel for an extended time, to take a break and gain perspective, if you're longing to see new things and experience different cultures, or to be with friends and have fun, seek adventure or just to relax, then that's where your focus should be. For as the (very true) saying goes: *Where attention goes, energy flows and result shows.*

Your Job or Career makes it Difficult to Travel

Are you worried that taking a long trip would make you uninteresting on the job market and ruin your career? That you'll never find another job again and your family will starve? That employers will think you're too adventurous or lazy having "just" been traveling for a whole year? That maybe you should postpone your travel dreams until you retire? Is it like a big mystery to you how people can just leave the Rat Race and do something totally different?

According to the Harris Poll, people (Americans that is, but we're sure they're not the only ones) are working harder than ever, putting in 100 – 200 more hours per year than their parents did.

And, as author and stress management expert Don Joseph Goewey says regarding this in his article, "Want your brain to make you brilliant? Give it a vacation":

"Those are averages; you might be working more than that. These extra hours are time away from our kids, friends, spouses, and even our bed. The Bureau of Labor Statistics says we sleep less than our parents did; one to two hours less. Vacation is a time to recoup that lost time and revitalize our minds and hearts."

We couldn't agree more!

51

The downside of our overworking lifestyle can also be seen very clearly in the morbidity and mortality statistics. The #1 killer is not the same as it was a hundred years ago, when most people died from bacterial and viral infections, as well as childbirth for women. The #1 killer today is stress related diseases. Don Joseph continues:

"If we go about it correctly, a vacation can break the negative cycle and renew us in ways that can make the upcoming year less stressful."

But you know this already don't you? That to take some time off from everyday stress makes you feel so much better. To know is one thing though, to do is something completely different!

And here's where the Buts set in. "But I can't just leave my job," "I don't have enough money" or "I don't have the time" for example. At a first glance, this might be true but if you take a deeper look at your situation, there's usually something you can do to change things around regarding your job, or to create the money as well as the time. Often it's about seeing what's important in your life and start prioritizing, like your health, your family, your future,

But being in a stressful mode can make it more difficult to see clearly. Here's Don Joseph Goewey again:

"Stress hormones also hyper-activate the brain's fear center producing Type-A behavior and locking our brain into "threat mode." This neurotoxic brain state tends to interpret any uncertainty as a threat to our survival. When you think I can't afford to take time off, it's usually the brain's fear center thinking for you. It's the brain using you, instead

of you using the brain. You need to reset the brain to peace, which is the neuroplastic state that rebuilds and restores higher brain function. Vacation is a good way to reset the brain to peace"

This is something we have been convinced about for years. We have seen so many examples of this, how people take some time off and then come back, relaxed as well as full of energy and new ideas and set off to a much more successful life than they ever could have imagined.

And today, extended travel is increasingly recognized as a valuable experience and more and more people put their travel experience on their résumé. Employers are starting to realize that long term travel is not an escape and just a waste of time, quite the opposite.

Furthermore, are you one of those whose working situation is no longer right for you? Does your job or career no longer excite you and give you the stimulation it once did? Do you feel less alive and enthusiastic than you once did about your work? Does your picture of where you want to be, and where you actually are, fail to match up precisely? Or have you been laid off and don't know which way to choose from here?

There are natural cycles of up and downs in our lives, working lives included. Sometimes you feel stuck and don't know what steps to take to get into the flow again. This can be a perfect time to just leave the old and start something new. It's a perfect way to get a perspective on your career as well as on your life in general. Spending time away from home and from your job will make it possible for you to review what you have done so far, to get an update on what your opportunities are and to create a base for taking you to the next level in your work life. And actually, it doesn't have to be career or travel. It can be both!

Long ago in Morocco, North Africa. Our first "exotic" stop sign

Another interesting sign we found, South Island New Zealand

Magnus shopping for breakfast in Yuma, Arizona, USA

Maria shopping for breakfast in Cochin, Kerala, Southern India

The advantages of traveling in this situation (well, always) are many and on many levels:

1. You leave your work responsibilities: This gives you the opportunity to let go of your obligations and the mind set of your specific field (and of course also gives you time to relax generally).

2. You expose yourself to new environments: As you let go of old ways, you expose yourself to new environments, new people and new ideas to fill up the old space. You are more open to new things than when you are at home focusing on familiar problems and patterns, things that don't require you to think outside the box.

3. You practice and learn many skills: You get to practice and learn many skills that can be of great value when you come back and return to your old work situation - or create a new one. Traveling will provide you with lots of opportunities to develop in many areas:

- You'll be sure to strengthen your capabilities to be more flexible, to plan, to organize and to negotiate.
- You'll improve your ability to be self sufficient and to improvise.
- You'll learn to understand and deal with people from different backgrounds and from different cultures.
- You can learn new languages.

Not to mention the globalization of the economy and the increased cultural and ethnical diversity where international experience is of great importance. Long term travel can actually be a fantastic business asset and a perfect investment in your career! Some people even plan their trip with their career in mind.

Consider things like:

- What skills do you want to improve?
- What do you want to learn along the way?
- Are there any special people you want to meet?
- Seminars you'd like to attend somewhere in the world?
- Potential business areas you'd like to study?
- Exhibitions or museums to visit?
- Languages to learn?
- Would Volunteering be something for you?

You could make your trip the perfect stepping stone to take your career to the next level or to start a new one.

Leave of Absence or Quit...

To take a sabbatical from your job can be done in different ways. You can of course quit, but taking a leave of absence, with or without pay, is also an option to consider. What policy does your company have for taking long breaks? Do they have a policy at all, or could you be the reason they create one?

A friend of ours wanted to travel for six months with his family and asked his company for permission. They didn't have any policy for people taking time off to travel – nobody had ever asked! They do now though – and it did allow our friend to go on that trip!

Today more and more companies are open to their employees taking some extended time off. It's well known that happy, relaxed, enthusiastic and inspired workers do a better job and are more motivated to stay with their employers. It's also usually far easier for a company if they can keep their old employees rather than having to find new ones.

And if you are worried about your career, consider our friend who took six months off to travel with his family. The company he worked for wouldn't let him go in the first place but when he threatened to quit completely they agreed. He just wouldn't take no for an answer. Funnily enough, upon his return he was offered a promotion! It turned out that the six months off that he couldn't get at first turned out to be a great career move!

Even if you have your own company, traveling for an extended time can be both possible and an advantage. A while ago we interviewed Ed Gillespie, co-founder of the communication agency Futerra, who took a one year sabbatical from running the company. Some of the advantages with having been away from his company for so long were, as he says, that he came back "being more productive, with a cool head and a fresh pair of eyes."

Maybe you have a job that could be done from anywhere? Then it might also be a possibility to bring it along with you, or parts of it, and continue to do some work along the way. Or maybe you can rearrange your job and do a more "travel friendly" version of it during your sabbatical.

A little warning though: with all the new impressions and ideas you'll have acquired and the growth that you'll experience while away, your old job may not even be interesting to you when you get back! Maybe it's time to get a new one. Like the Norwegian author, Jo Nesbø, for example. He was so overworked that he just demanded a six month leave. Getting back to the office after six months he just realized that working there was not what he wanted to do. He wanted to write a book and was not going to be like his father who also dreamed of writing a book after retiring but died before he was able to. So, Jo followed his dream, quit his job and started to write bestselling books.

You can of course also simply quit your job to be able to travel. Remember, quitting is not only the end of something; it's also the beginning of something else. If you know you don't have your old job waiting for you when you get back, you'll also be especially receptive to new ideas and possibilities that you meet along the way.

There are innumerable examples of businesses that have been started from ideas that people have had while they were traveling. Dietrich Mateschitz from Austria discovered when he traveled in Thailand that people were drinking a special drink to feel uplifted and get more energy. He took it to Europe and it is now selling around the world under the name "Red Bull", the world's most famous energy drink. Dietrich himself has become a billionaire.

Another example is Paul Morrison and Lyn Hughes who loved to travel. During a long boring flight from England to South America they sketched out a magazine that would contain everything they themselves would like to find in a travel magazine. From their home, they then started Wanderlust, today one of the world's leading travel magazines for independent and adventurous travelers.

For us as well, we have had all of our best business ideas when we have been away from home on some journey. Ideas and contacts that we have brought with us and that have become a new fresh start (or continuation) for us and also have turned out to be an inspiration to many people in our country. We have been exposed to many new ideas that we wouldn't have experienced if we'd been just staying at home.

We started our first business after having been inspired in a shop in Germany. The shop sold fantastic organic clothes of very high quality. We really loved these products and realized they didn't exist at that time at home in Sweden. When we started our organic company with these things as the core product, we were the first ones in Sweden and we really got a lot of attention (and followers). So, you never know where some traveling can take you!

You'd Love to Take a Long Trip but Your Children are in School

If you have children and especially children of school age, it's not uncommon to see this as a big obstacle for your dream to travel for a longer time. How could it be possible to just take the kids out of school for several months? What about their education? Their friends?

You might worry that taking a long term trip will ruin their chances of getting a good education. Or that taking them out of school may lead them to falling behind? Or maybe you think that being away for a longer period will make your children feel lonely and they risk losing their friends? And without their friends, will they get bored all the time and ruin the whole trip? And just imagine how you will be feeling, years from now, if they in any way suffer because you were so egotistical that you took them traveling the world instead of letting them stay at home and get a proper education.

If you don't think about it too deeply, it's very common to believe that school is the only place where our children learn about life. But if you reflect on it a little more you realize that it's just not so.

What is the meaning of education in the first place? As we see it, the meaning of education is to learn about the world we live in. How to survive and function in it. How to socialize and cooperate with its people, and how to make it a better place. The most common scenario for learning is sitting indoors in a room all day together with twenty or thirty other children of the same age, from the same social background, with one adult whose task it is to teach you about the world and the essentials of life. And even though the school system has its function and many teachers do a fantastic job, school is not the only place to learn about life.

Another scenario could be out in the world itself, gathering first hand experiences. Meeting with different people and seeing new places and learning about them. To learn things like socialization, communication, social studies, geography, languages and history, (well, most things) traveling is fantastic! Consider everything you can learn just from what's around you in different places: history and architecture, natural science; animals, climates, time zones, oceans, beaches, deserts, volcanoes, currencies, exchange rates, aerodynamics/planes, boats, ships, trains, food, music, art.... not to mention people who tell you about their lives or share their special interests.

"Do not let school get in the way of a good education"
- Loesje

There's so much to learn from the everyday life in a different culture. So many things that invite you to be curious and the acquiring of knowledge when you travel is enormous. When you travel around in the world, you learn about these things with all your senses. You can hear the sounds, see things with your own eyes, smell the wonderful (or awful) smells, taste the different foods, and feel all the different temperatures.

You collect experiences which become one with you and help you get references to your life. To have felt in your body how big a Redwood tree is and how much you actually have to look up to be able to see the top, compared to looking at a picture of the tree in a book or seeing it on TV. Or looking at the stars in Australia and wonder where you're favorite ones are. The Big Dipper replaced by the Southern Cross, a constellation which is also illustrated on the Australian flag. To experience how long it actually takes to go from Chicago to Seattle on a train, or from Sweden to Southern Spain in a car. To feel your insignificance when you compare yourself to the humpback whale swimming next to the boat... or to learn that your new friends in India pay as much (or as little) in house tax for a whole year as you pay for an ice cream at home.

These are a few of the things our own children (and we adults too) have experienced and learned from. Maybe the most important lesson of all is learning that we are sharing this world with a lot of other people who, on the outside, can appear different from us, but upon looking closer, we see that we are rather alike and have a whole lot in common.

Traveling also allows children to get a view of the world that they can't get at home. It gives them the opportunity to see with their own eyes what things look like, compared to other people's pictures that are delivered to them in books and in the media.

"There's not just only one way that's the right way"
- Mamma Mu, famous Swedish cow

So, there are lots of ways to acquire knowledge; the classroom is not a place with a monopoly of learning possibilities. Learning can take place all the time everywhere. Traveling enables you to open your mind and learn in new ways and the learning that takes place while experiencing the world is massive.

Another thing to consider is the many learning opportunities there are in making preparations for a long term trip. To be part of the planning process of a big trip is an experience worthy of any school project. Like studying and gathering information about different places, setting goals and working towards those goals as well as helping to create the money you need to be able to make a reality of it all. A child old enough to be part of that process will have many resources to draw from when later doing all kinds of projects at school (and in life in general) and when you are on the road there are things happening that you can't plan. Challenges undoubtedly turn up and give you even more possibilities to learn and to strengthen your problem solving muscles.

"His perspective of the world has broadened, his vocabulary has increased, he has learned more languages, become more brave, more social, more self confident, more everything."
- Lydia, mother, world traveler, TV journalist and friend, about traveling with her son.

Another dimension of traveling as a child is all the advantages you get from these experiences in the future. Adults take a career break and get new energy, a new perspective and learn new things that they benefit from when they get back home. In the same way a break can serve children as well, in both their future studies and working life. And, as the world is getting smaller, international experiences become more and more of an advantage.

"Experience of living abroad as a child is the single best predictor of success in an international career as an adult."
- Edward Hasbrouck, Travel Guru

What About Socialization?

It's not uncommon to be concerned about the children's social life when you're thinking about traveling. And if you believe that a child's social life must consist of being part of a group of twenty or thirty other children of the same age every day, traveling might be a bit tricky (if you don't choose a school abroad of course). If, on the other hand, you look upon socialization as the ability to be with different kinds of people, children as well as teenagers and adults, people from different cultures and social levels and who speak different languages, then traveling can provide innumerable ways to improve your social abilities and create friends for life from all corners of our planet

"The whole world is his home. My son is used to many different ways of living. His ability to adjust to different cultures and languages has made him an urbane and interesting person with good self esteem. I think he sees more possibilities than most people his age."
- Lovisa, world traveling single mother and friend

Regarding socialization, it can be difficult to leave a best friend for a long period. But then, the relationship can perhaps continue on another level. You can send postcards and letters to each other. You'll also have a reason to practice writing and the friend will probably be very excited to receive greetings from exotic places around the world. Today, you can even continue to talk to each other daily from most places, thanks to the internet and very cheap or even free telephone calls or instant chat programs. And maybe the friend can come and visit and travel with you and be part of the journey for a while? This can give the relationship even more dimensions – new experiences to share when you get back home. To travel with children is a fantastic opportunity full of possibilities to learn about infinite amounts of different things, and sometimes, things that seemed so big and important, like studying for a test at home, may look like a very small detail compared to all there is to learn out in the world.

The question is not whether you dare to take your child out of school to travel, but whether you should dare not to do it!

More Ways to Handle the School Issue when Traveling

There are many ways to handle the school issue depending on different things.

- How long you are traveling for?
- How are you traveling; will you be staying in one place or travel around?
- How old is the child?
- How open minded is the child's teacher at home to different ways of learning?
- How open minded are you yourself to these things?

If you will stay for a long period in one area, you can enroll your child in a local, or, if there is one, an international school. We have friends who have done this for periods as short as four weeks so you don't necessarily have to be staying for months in the same place. If "proper schooling" is important to you, this might be an option.

Another alternative is to enroll your child, temporarily or permanently, in a distance school. Here, you can get plans for learning outside of the classroom and you get materials and tests and all the help and support both the child and you as a parent might want. The number of distance schools is increasing all the time and if you are English speaking, there's a big number to choose from.

Yet another way, probably the most common, is to create your own schedule together with the child's teacher at home. You can then be in contact with the school for questions and support. To send in material and tests is not a big deal in today's computerized world. You don't even have to drag books and things around the world. It is usually possible to find some kind of internet café even in the most remote places where you can surf for information and download and print material.

We also want to add here, that helping your child to learn doesn't have to be a big thing. It is something you as a parent normally do every day in different ways. Depending on the child's age, you may have to support it with organizing and structuring their schoolwork and to be there to help find answers. You certainly don't need to know everything about all the school subjects yourself to be able to support your child with their school work. The tricky thing with educating children is when you have many from different circumstances and at different levels and you have to teach all of them the same things at the same time. For that, it can be a help to be a trained teacher but teaching your own child is often easier than you imagine. Tuition becomes individualized and very effective. Your "pupil" will get 100% attention and you can usually cover in about an hour what takes a whole day at school to accomplish.

For us, the school question hasn't required any specific attention when we've been traveling since we've home schooled permanently. We haven't needed to ask anyone for permission to take our children for longer trips or to discuss with a teacher what they'll have to learn when they are away. As homeschoolers our children have simply continued with their normal way of learning but in different environments.

As support for our home schooling we have used an American school that offers a home school program. They work with families all over the world and their program goes all the way up through high school. Our oldest children now have their high school diplomas from there. You can find out more about it at www.Clonlara.org

Travel With Kids – Challenge or Opportunity?

Traveling with kids, or traveling as a family, can for some seem like the ultimate challenge. To others, like ourselves, it's just the greatest of opportunities for learning and growing together. Traveling together for a long time gives you the opportunity to get to know your family members and to see who they really are. In many families today, you don't know your members very well. You spend so much time away from each other, at work, school, at different activities and when you get home, you sit in front of the computer or the TV. And then, what's left? How much time do you have every day to connect to and communicate with your spouse and your kids?

When we talk to people about this, we realize that many are concerned that spending a lot of time with their family would make them go crazy. Maybe they'd even come back ready for a divorce?

What we've found in reality though, it's usually the opposite. When you go on an extended journey, you leave most of the different sources of everyday stress at home. You get rid of the things that stand between yourself and the other members of your family: all the stuff, the activities, the obligations. What you have left is just yourselves and your adventure. Now you have the time to see who this person you sometimes meet in the hallway on your way out really is.

When you travel, you will be away together in new unknown places and situations. You'll create new circumstances that can help you to break old negative patterns and habits that are connected to your life at home. You will experience lots of interesting things together. You will get plenty of opportunities to practice cooperating with each other since problem solving is a natural gift of every long term trip.

And sometimes, the road just isn't easy to walk and the sun isn't shining and things aren't very fun, but this will be part of your journey together too and oftentimes, the "worst" situations are the one's that'll create your warmest memories.

To do some long term travel with kids and spouse is just so different to being at home and if you haven't done it, it can be really difficult to imagine what a "boost" for your family life it can provide.

So, what's your family life like? How would you like it to be? Imagine yourself twenty years from now. What kind of memories would you want to share with your wife/husband and your children?

When you travel with kids and go out into the world, there are a few things which are good to keep in mind:

Take your time and travel slowly. Don't be in a hurry. Be very generous with the time you reserve for both your travels as well as your stays. Also, trying to cram in as much as possible to see and do may not be the best starting position for a relaxed and fun family journey.

Adjust to the kid's age. It is a totally different thing, to travel with an older teenager or with a newborn - and with one child or four. The younger the kids, and the more there are of them, the slower the pace we recommend. Really young children can keep themselves busy and be fascinated by small everyday things and you can take the opportunity yourself to learn from them and experience the world from this perspective. The older they get the more you'll of course be able to communicate about what you want to do and where you'll want to go. You'll have plenty of opportunities to practice communication and negotiation, or consensus, skills. And we mean that! See it as a way to strengthen both your kids' and your own abilities to listen and to be considerate as well as to express your desires.

Be in the present. This is also something you can learn more about from your kids and, the younger they are, the better they can teach you. Traveling and being away from all the musts and shoulds is the perfect time to practice mindfulness and just taking in what is. This is also the best way to keep kids calm and relaxed (not to mention yourself). And don't worry, your trip won't be uneventful and boring, rather the opposite (and you can be sure that all kinds of unexpected, unimaginable things will show up). You'll learn how fascinating even the smallest thing can be and you'll experience how it is to feel really alive.

Remember that "the journey is the goal." Well, this is very connected to the ability to be in the present. When you focus on and take in the here and now, you realize that everything that happens along the trip is part of your journey, not just the end destination some two or four or seven months ahead. And everything that happens along the way, all of it, that's what the journey is about.

These are things we have been taught ourselves by our kids when we have been traveling with them and the more we have been able to follow this, the more relaxed and fun our trips have been.

So to travel with kids can really be an opportunity to learn to live your life in the best of ways and of course, this approach does not have to stop when your trip is over. We think it's a real advantage to be able to live in a more mindful way in our times whether you are traveling the world or staying home dealing with your everyday business.

Of Course You Want to Travel but Your Friends and Family Will Have Lots to Say About it

One of the most common concerns we have when we want to make a decision about something a bit "different", is what other people will say. Taking a long term trip is something many consider out of the ordinary. It's not totally uncommon for travelers or would-be travelers to be met with different kinds of criticism from people who are close to them.

This is a challenge which can limit the realization of your dreams more than you may think. You might hear things like: "Should you really quit your job, don't you have any idea what the job market looks like these days?" Or maybe, "So, how will you be able to support your family when you get back totally broke?" Another one might be: "How can you even think of taking your children out of school to go traveling, what if they fall behind or lose all their friends?" Whereas some well meaning people may focus more on: "How are you going to cope with all the diseases that are out there and have you really considered the risks of terrorist attacks?" And, by the way, questions like this may not only come from people around you, they can also be asked by someone even more close to you – yourself.

Taking a new step, or stepping a little differently to most people, can awaken all kinds of fears in people (and in yourself). Close relatives may think they will never see you again. Friends may be afraid of losing a good friend. People may start to think that they are not enough fun or interesting to be with. They can also feel confronted with questions about their own lives. They may start to think about whether they themselves really are living the life they want and should they also make some changes, do something they've long desired? Or, are they really doing all they can for their children? Or, should they really stay another year in their old boring job?

When someone close to us does something out of the ordinary it can be very inspiring, but for some people it can also feel like a threat. It can force us to look at our own life. And if we are not prepared and willing to do that, it's not uncommon to react with some kind of defense against this new either by saying or doing things that we hope will keep life unaltered. Something that makes us not have to confront this new situation that we think is too much for us. It's not actually about being mean but more a natural reaction to the fear of change. For a would-be traveler who might be a little sensitive to what people around him thinks, it can be quite discouraging though.

So what can you do when you suddenly experience yourself discouraged by the people that surround you? Here are some suggestions if (when!) you meet dream stealers who tell you everything you can't do, aren't capable of, or what's not appropriate, responsible or realistic:

1. *Remember, your trip (and your life) is for you, not for them.* Remember that they are probably afraid of something, and should you let their fear (even though it's well meaning) stand in the way for who you want to be and what you want to do? Instead, make a reality of your dream and show them what's possible. If you can do it, they can do it! Maybe they need a longer time to get in contact with, or start acting on their dreams; maybe a whole lifetime. Be an example and realize that whatever you dream about and whatever people say, they'll be affected by it. Besides, the people who want to keep you in your place, are they really such great role models? How do they live themselves? Are they happy people who live a life you would like to live? Are their advice and ideas something you really want to follow?

2. *Show those around you that you have made a decision.* Make it clear to them that you understand they want what's best for you. Also make it clear that what you want to do is based on a conscious decision, that it's something really important to you and that you would appreciate to get their support on this. To really "go public" with what you intend and let people know you're serious about it will also help to convince yourself that it's real and that you are serious about it.

3. *Make people part of your trip (those you want to).* If there are people who are close to you and who you want a continuing good relationship with, see if you can engage them in some way. Ask them to help you with something that has to do with your trip. Help them feel that they are needed and important. But, at the same time, beware not to load them with lots of boring everyday things to do while you're away and having the time of your life.

4. **Don't let people take your dream away from you!** Stick to it and remember why you wanted to go in the first place. This is something to ask yourself when you feel discouraged. Furthermore, surround yourself with people and things which help you to be in contact with and strengthen your dream.

"The kindergarten teacher told me he'd never be able to manage the school routine if he didn't get accustomed to it now. Relatives called me irresponsible… It requires good role models and strong focus not to get trapped in such destructive discussions"
- Lydia, world traveler, TV-journalist and friend (about traveling with her son when he was young)

Meet and/or read about people who have traveled, who travel and people who follow their hearts. Get some role models for what you want to do. Watch films and read books and magazines that are in line with what you want to do and who you want to be. And remember, you're the one who'll regret not going for your dream, not them.

"If a little dreaming is dangerous, the cure for it is not to dream less, but to dream more, to dream all the time."
- Marcel Proust

What a fantastic tree! A redwood in Northern California, USA

The ferry ride to Vancouver Island, BC, Canada is really breathtaking

We've spent lots of time on the fantastic beach in Byron Bay, Australia

Australia Zoo, we even met the legendary Steve "Crikey" Irwin!

You're afraid of Being a Victim of Crime, Violence or Terrorism

When you start to think about making that dream trip of yours a reality, it's not unusual to suddenly come up with lots of reasons why you shouldn't do it.

We have an instinctive fear of change and the unknown that may have the benefit of protecting us from the dangers of misadventure. At home, in our familiar environment, we're not exposed to lots of uncertainties but as we get ready to embark on something new and a bit different, the fears start to show up.

You start to notice scary things out there in the unfamiliar world. And if your area of fear is crime and violence (we all have our different concerns), that's what your worries will be about.

You might scare yourself with concerns about being a victim of violence or being robbed. Or by having thoughts like "in these times of terrorism, how will I ever feel safe traveling around in the world?" Or maybe "What if there's a riot in a place I'll be visiting?" Or even "With so much trouble in the world, how can I be sure nothing will happen to me?"

Of course there is crime and violence in the world, probably in your own environment as well. When you're in your familiar surroundings though, you know what to do, how to act, where to go and where not to go, and maybe you feel a bit more familiar with the people that surround you.

If this concern is something that's preying on your mind, there are things you can do. One is choosing to travel in areas of the world where you feel safe. Another thing you can do is to educate yourself.

In travel books and on travel sites you can immerse yourself in information and advice on everything from how to behave in different situations and different places around the world to stay safe, to what's the best lock to put on your backpack.

To talk to people who have done a lot of traveling, and hear about their experiences, is also something that we always recommend.

It is also worth noticing that most violence happens between people who know each other. And the place where you run the biggest risk of being a victim of violence is in your own home (especially if you are a woman or child).

Another thing you can do is to stop watching the TV news and reading newspapers. Since the focus in the media is primarily on "the bad things" in the world, it's easy to get discouraged and start thinking that the best and safest thing to do is to stay at home.

It's important to remember, though, that we seldom see headlines about all the fantastic, marvelous and positive things that happen around the world every day, every minute and every second!

If you're really concerned and want to increase your self confidence in this area, you could even take a course in self defense. Most probably, you will never have to use what you learn, but if it helps you feel safer, and better able to travel, it can be worth considering.

Also, the most common crimes that affect travelers are different forms of economic crime. Someone thinks that you have more than you need and wants to have a piece of it…

We remember ourselves, with happy embarrassment, one time when we were in southern Spain on our way across the border to Gibraltar. A man with great authority stepped up to our car and put a piece of paper under our windscreen wiper and announced that it was something we needed to be allowed across the border and told us the price. We gladly paid only to realize, when the person had quickly disappeared, that the important paper was just an old lottery ticket....

Fear of being a victim of a terrorist action is something that has become more common during recent years and of course, terrorism does exist. And the same goes for other anxieties such as disease, crime, accidents. The question is, how big are the risks really and are they a good reason to stay at home and avoid doing things you like and want to do?

"Conflict… what if we are both right?"
- Loesje

By the way, is home safer? As we have seen, bad things can happen everywhere.

There are of course areas and places in the world that are considered more risky and places that are considered safer, so if this is something that worries you, why not choose your destination accordingly?

You can, for example, find updated recommendations at each country's Foreign Office and you can check on the internet if you want to study this in detail. Lots of information can also be found on these pages:

http://travel.state.gov/travel/travel_1744.html
http://www.fco.gov.uk/en/travelling-and-living-overseas/

And remember, our world is big and there are an inordinate number of fantastic places to experience and in most of them you probably won't need to be worried about these issues for a second.

Furthermore, this is an area where we really think that it's more important to focus on solutions instead of the problem.

That may mean not giving in to fear, which, as we see it, is the reason that this problem exists in the first place.

"Fear makes strangers of people who would be friends."
- Shirley MacLaine

Traveling gives us fantastic opportunities to meet people from different cultures, religions, and social strata. Meeting people in real life is a great way to see and realize that behind these and other superficial differences like color, language, clothing and living circumstances, we are all rather alike.

We all have the same basic needs and values. We need food to eat and a safe place to live. We want to love and to be loved. We want to take care of our families and friends and we want to be happy.

"Perhaps travel cannot prevent bigotry, but by demonstrating that all people cry, laugh, eat, worry and die, it can introduce the idea, that if we try and understand each other, we may even become friends."
- Maya Angelou

We are bombarded all the time with pictures and opinions from the media and from our surroundings which can easily make us think that people and places foreign to us are something to be afraid of, something that may be a threat to us or something we must protect ourselves against.

When you travel and become friends with people on the other side of the world (or in a neighboring country or maybe even in your own) you quickly realize how much we have in common.

We are all human beings and the more of us who have a chance to experience that, the bigger the chance that we will be able to live without thinking we have to fight each other. Who wants to kill a friend?

Or as travel guru Edward Hasbrouk says it:

"At the end of the day, our safety and security depend most of all on understanding the world – understanding that is the result, above all else, of the direct personal contact, experiences and learning that result from international travel."

You're Terrified of Flying

"What if something goes wrong with the plane (which it probably will)?"

"What if I panic somewhere over the Atlantic and want to get off?"

"How will I be able to let unfamiliar people take my life in their hands as I must if put myself on a plane? How will I know they're competent enough?"

"How will I be able to enjoy a long term trip around the world when my mind will be busy all the time thinking about the next flight?"

These are questions you might be familiar with if you (like I, Maria, used to be) are a person who sees flying as one of the most horrifying activities you can expose yourself to.

Fear of flying is something that holds many people back from going out into the world and although travel by no means has to involve flying, for most people going on a long distance trip does include some use of air transport.

Intellectually we can rationalize that the most dangerous means of transport by far is the car, and one of the safest ways, if not THE safest, is to fly. Unfortunately, our fears are more deeply rooted than our reason can contend with.

"Nothing is so much to be feared as fear"
- Loesje

Often we can't explain why we are frightened, only that we are, so we cannot use reason to overcome those fears.

Our fear of flying may have little to do with flight itself but may be triggered by air travel.

I, Maria, took my first trip by plane almost fifty years ago (time flies!) I then continued to fly around the world without ever feeling any kind of anxiety. In fact, I really enjoyed it. Then, I had my first child. All of a sudden, just the thought of being confined in something high up in the sky, with my life in the hands of someone I didn't know, and could not even see, made me absolutely terrified. I didn't fly for many years. It wasn't even an option to consider.

We traveled a lot as a growing family but never by plane.

We traveled by car, train or boat. We really got to learn the geography of Europe, where we did most of our traveling. One day the rest of the family started talking about going somewhere "far away," and I knew the time had come when I had to do something about my fear of flying.

I signed up for a three day "fear of flying" course and that was the turning point. To meet with people in the same situation and learn about both the psychology and the mechanics of flying, gave me so many insights and so much information that I just had to surrender. I began to let go of my fears and even started to look forward to some renewed traveling.

We then booked tickets for the whole family to go on a six month trip around the world. And this time we were going to do a lot of flying!

The first flight was a bit shaky but I practiced everything I had learned in the course and it all went very well. After a few trips, we one day was on a flight between Fiji and New Zealand, and, for the first time in years, I found myself enjoying it!

Being able to fly again has given me, and the rest of the family, so many opportunities to see fantastic places and meet wonderful people that I'm really glad I took some action and confronted my fear.

As an extra bonus it has helped me to be less frightened in other situations as well. I am generally more daring now. It has helped me realize that many of the things I have been afraid of haven't been dangerous at all; they were just notions that had existed in my mind.

Of course, to do some extended world travel, you don't necessarily have to fly. There are many other forms of transportation to choose from and your journey will be something different if flying isn't in your program. But if you do want to travel and fly and are avoiding it because of fear, you too can turn that around, I'm sure!

"For years, fear of flying prevented me from going out into the world, what's your excuse?"

The Most Fundamental– HEALTH

Health issues, or rather the fear of acquiring some acute or exotic disease, or of becoming ill or involved in an accident in an unfamiliar environment, is a "biggie" for many travelers and potential travelers.

"What if I get ill in the middle of nowhere and there are no doctors around"? What if my kid gets sick? Can I really expect to get proper health care in a foreign country? I catch cold if anyone so much as sneezes, how would I survive out in the world with all the known and unknown diseases? "What if there's an accident and I am taken care of by people who may not be qualified?

If these are the kinds of questions you ask yourself when you're talking about traveling, there are many things you can do to make yourself feel safer. For example, you could start with a health check up with your doctor or health practitioner. Knowing that you are fit and healthy is a good way to start and also gives you the opportunity to discuss your health worries and get some advice. This is especially important if you already have a specific health issue that needs attending to.

The same goes for your teeth. Knowing that your teeth are in good condition is reassuring, especially if you want to travel to a part of the world where you would prefer not having to visit the dentist!

A good thing, whether or not you are concerned about health issues, is to educate yourself about the conditions and the environment you are traveling to.

You'll find plenty of information on this subject on the Internet. You can, for example, find updated recommendations at each country's Foreign Offices. Here are two good ones with plenty of information for worldwide travel.

http://travel.state.gov/travel/travel_1744.html
http://www.fco.gov.uk/en/travelling-and-living-overseas/

If there are any specific diseases you worry about, or are concerned about a special area of the world, a good thing to do is to educate yourself about the situation.

You can research facts like:

- Where is the disease – in the whole country you want to visit or in certain areas?
- Is it a year-round problem or only during a certain time of the year?
- How can you protect yourself, are there preventive actions you can take?
- What can you do if you become affected?
- And also, what is the real risk?

Furthermore, if you find out a risk really is bigger than you feel comfortable with, why not choose another destination or another form of traveling? The possibilities are endless!

For additional help to feel safe and make it easier to let go of focusing on accidents and health risks, one option is to participate in a "First Aid" course. Doing this will strengthen your self confidence for travel whether you are planning a trip to somewhere exotic or whether you are thinking of exploring closer to home.

And if you dream about some adventurous travel, you may even consider something like a "First Aid Wilderness" course to give your self confidence a boost.

Our Experience

We have, luckily, not been affected by any major illnesses or accidents when we have been away. The worst was actually when Magnus got pneumonia once when we were traveling around Europe in our campervan. We rented an apartment and stayed there for a few weeks until he got fit to travel again. The big advantage with that was that we got the opportunity to explore the beautiful city Nice in southern France, thoroughly and that it helped him quit smoking easily and quickly! We have also visited hospitals in different locations like Spain (where it is totally free for us as tourists!) when Viktoria stepped on a sea urchin and Aurora hurt her knee and needed a cast. We have visited a very interesting hospital in southern India when we suspected that Aurora had got malaria. It turned out that she hadn't, but people were so helpful in every way and it was really a memorable experience. Another time we all got a bad cold, also in India, and the hotel we were staying in at that time had their own doctor, whom we could consult, free of charge. He gave us ayurvedic remedies that made us all well in a flash.

We have also suffered from the absolute most common travel related "disease:" traveler's stomach. We've had it twice - after we visited other sick families. It happened in France and in Canada! On the other hand, when we've been spending time in more exotic places like India and Northern Africa we've remained perfectly healthy the whole time!

We have also been careless enough to gain experience with the second most common traveler's complaint – sun burn. We have now learned that going snorkeling on the day you arrive in an exotic sunny location, without sufficient protection (high SPF sunscreen and/or long sleeve t-shirts and pants) is not a very good idea if you want to be able to sit comfortably during the day or rest comfortably in bed at night.

Mistakes are great moments – at least in retrospect :)

If you are faced with a health issue when you're away, don't hesitate to consult a local health practitioner. Usually they know a lot about illnesses that are common in that specific part of the world and you also get the opportunity to get some new perspective on medicine and health care. We have realized this is an area where many people are especially concerned and feel unsure when they are in foreign surroundings. We once had the idea that Sweden has the best healthcare in the world and nowhere else are doctors so qualified and reliable. We know better now. You can of course find qualified health practitioners all over the world, both more traditional ones as well as the ones who are more into alternative therapies. So, being open to look at things in new ways, as well as trying new ways of treating things, can really be a positive experience and broaden your view on health and health care.

You Can Get Ill Anytime, Anywhere...

Most commonly though you become ill when you're in your home environment. Often the reason is too much stress and worry, things that can affect your health both more acutely as well as in more chronic ways.

As we see it, stress, worry, and living an uninspiring life are considerably bigger risk factors for coming down with a serious illness than a relaxing, adventurous, long term journey around the world.

So remember: taking it easy, having fun and relaxing are things that can affect your immune system in a positive way. It's also good to strive for a healthy lifestyle in general and be clear about what you personally need to be physically and mentally fit. Good basic health is never a disadvantage, and something that will benefit you on your trip as well as in the rest of your life.

This, together with some common sense, will definitely take you a long way (maybe even further than both vaccinations and medicines.)

And when you have learned everything you can, and been on your dream trip and are back safe and happy, you can even be a role model for other people who want to do the same and don't think they can!

So, don't let fear get in your way

With regard to all the different fears we may have that prevent us from going out into the world and do the things we are dreaming about, take a look at what fear or fears you associate with traveling.

Study that specific area, gather facts, read about it, and talk to people who have experience of it. Learn how you can prepare yourself, how you can protect yourself and consider if it is really a risk at all.

And remember – just because you are afraid of something does not make it dangerous.

Just think of how many people are terrified at the very thought of getting up on a stage and speaking in front of an audience. It may feel terrifying, yes, but that doesn't mean that it's dangerous.

Also, if you work with these things and still find yourself afraid, you can always choose to take the step and make your journey anyway, because, as the saying goes:

Courage is to feel the fear and do it anyway.

Finally we just want to pass on what Wade from Vagabondjourney.com had to say on this subject in an interview we made with him, since we found it very clever:

"Everything always works out. The great thing about leaving is that you can usually return to the same place where you are standing right now. Have faith that you will figure everything out when you need to, and rest your mind about planning. Nothing ever works out according to plan anyway, so why waste the mental energy bothering with it. The adverse consequences of traveling that you may foresee are merely illusions. You are not nearly wise enough to foresee the future, so stop trying — go forth and see what happens.

It is my impression that the human capacity for planning for the future is a very rudimentary development that usually only serves to provoke fear and to hamstring any desire that we may have for change. If anyone thinks about their future they get scared — "what if this happens, what if that happens." You know what? "What ifs" rarely ever really happen. Humans tend to be intelligent enough to make the most of their situations when they are in the moment, and often have the ability to sidestep any "what ifs" when they need to be sidestepped. You will be alright.

Fear is an emotion that is reserved for the potential occurrence of future adversity. When in a moment of adversity, fear is rarely ever felt. I know that I have often felt fear about future possibilities — about being robbed, about getting lost, being cold etc . . — but every time I have been in such a circumstance, fear is the last thing that I felt, as I was much too busy focusing on how to get out of the bad situation to be scared. Fear is a survival instinct only in the fact that it keeps you sitting where you are, it keeps you way out of danger. When in a bad circumstance you automatically figure it out, and usually leave the moment saying, "Wow, that was not that bad after all."

When given free range, fear will keep you sitting right where you are forever and ever and ever. It is amazing that many people would rather be comfortable, hemmed in by fears of future occurrences, than to really find out what the future may hold. There are no "what ifs" in a moment of adversity, so why leave yourself hampered with "what ifs" when the horizon is clear and the sun is shining?"

Viktoria with fresh tea leaves at a tea factory in Kerala, Southern India

Some guys we met on the road in the hills in Kerala, India

Just back from shopping for the latest fashions, Mumbai, India

If You Want to Travel the World but Don't Think it's Possible, Start by Believing That it is!

You've probably heard the old refrain: "I'll believe it when I see it." As we see it, it's actually the other way around. You start by believing in something and it will, sooner or later, become a reality.

So if you have a desire to travel the world, try not to get stuck in all the reasons why it's not possible, instead play with the idea that it is. Dream about it, see in your head that you're already there; look at the scenery, listen to the sounds, see if you can even smell something special that you connect with your trip: the ocean, some food, a flower...

Also, talk about your trip. Not with people who'll discourage you and say things like you're unrealistic and irresponsible (you probably know them), but with people who will be traveling with you. Or talk to other world travelers. And don't forget to dream a bit about what you'll bring back home after you've traveled the world. What would you like to have learned? What would you love to see has changed when you come back as a "new" person?

Many times when we have traveled, or rather before we have gone away, we haven't had a clue how to sort everything out and make the trip possible but we have had this picture in our minds. We haven't always had the exact same picture, since there are five of us, but a similar vision. We have then talked about it, made the picture clearer, dreamed about it and, at one point, we have been ready to make the decision to go for it.

Then things start to fall into place! A house sitter turns up to stay in our home and take care of our cats. We get invited to stay at someone's house for free in the area where we want to go. We manage to create the money necessary to make it possible (even if we to start with had no idea how). There has always been a way.

There's a very famous quote that we think is very suitable when describing this phenomenon. Most of you have probably read or heard it before but we think it worth repeating:

"Until one is committed, there is hesitancy, the chance to draw back, always ineffectiveness. Concerning all acts of initiative (and creation), there is one elementary truth the ignorance of which kills countless ideas and splendid plans: that the moment one definitely commits oneself, the providence moves too. A whole stream of events issues from the decision, raising in one's favor all manner of unforeseen incidents, meetings and material assistance, which no man could have dreamt would have come his way. I learned a deep respect for one of Goethe's couplets: "Whatever you can do or dream you can, begin it. Boldness has genius, power and magic in it!"
- W. H. Murray in The Scottish Himalaya Expedition (quoting John Anster who in turn paraphrased Goethe's Faust in the final two sentences of the preceding quote from Murray).

And now that you have been looking into your particular "Buts" and maybe have an idea of what's stopping you, and hopefully some ideas about what you can do about it, think of the above quote as well.

Even if you haven't solved all your problems, even if there are a few challenges left in your life before you can start packing your suitcases and take off, start trusting that things will sort themselves out along the way.

There will always be parts that you can't control and you will never be totally "finished" or absolutely "ready." That's just life. But what you can do is start exercising your "trust muscle" and one of the best ways to do this is to commit. Commit to following your dream, to go for it, face your challenges and fears and start preparing for your life's trip and we promise you, providence will start to move!

6. How to Travel

We hope that you might be a bit clearer about some of your own Buts by now and hopefully you're also starting to realize that there are ways to overcome them. As a next step, it's really time to take a look at what you want your dream trip to be like! What would you like to do? How do you want to travel? How do you want to stay, and of course, where would you like to go?

Looking into different ways that you can travel will help you turn your dreams into a reality by giving you ideas and inspiration to start taking inspired actions in the direction of your trip. We like to talk about "the travel stew," some different areas you can look into to get a clearer picture of what your specific trip could look like according to your personal circumstances and preferences.

Our experience is that there are three main ingredients that create the foundation of your "dream travel stew" – DO, TRAVEL and STAY. These ingredients are all dependent on each other. If you're clear about these three it will take you a long way and help you to make clear decisions about your extended travel.

What do you want to DO?

It may sound like an obvious question, but to have clarity about what you want to do on your journey is fundamental. It will give you guidance on how to make a good travel mixture.

- Do you only want pure "pleasure" and relaxation?
- Do you want to be active and explore and discover new things?
- Do you want to make a difference and volunteer?
- Do you want to learn new skills or work?

How do you want to TRAVEL?

What means of transport will suit you the best? How you decide to travel will influence where you'll want to go and what you'll want to do.

- Do you want to fly, sail, drive, or ride a motorbike or even a bicycle?
- Does exploring in a motor home appeal to you?
- Maybe you just want to use your feet and walk?
- Do you want to be on the move or just stay in one place?

Where do you want to STAY?

It's also important to think about what kind of accommodations you desire and what will feel good to you. This also includes how you plan to solve the food issue.

- Are you considering hotels and restaurants or hostels and self-catering?
- Maybe a house exchange is an alternative for you?
- Have you ever thought about Network Traveling or using a Hospitality Organization?
- Do you have any special needs?

Make your mix

When you find a mixture of these three ingredients that feels right and excites you, you will most certainly have solved 80% of the question - "How Can I Travel?" The rest are minor adjustments that can be added along the way to give you the extra special touches to your travel experience.

With this said about the "how to travel," we once again want to emphasize the importance of why you want to go.

When you understand the "why" then you create the determination and desire to do it. Just because you know how to travel, does not automatically lead you to actually take off on your journey. If, on the other hand, you have a burning desire to go somewhere, you will most certainly start to find out how you can.

When we first started to dream about going on a long term trip, we had no idea how we would pull it off. We were quite sure that we wanted to do something and that we wanted to travel for a long time. In those days the kids where young and we didn't want to drag them around on endless flights, even less, we didn't want to go by car and stay at hotels or hostels and different places all the time. We came up with several ideas, but nothing felt really good. Then one day, an old friend called. We hadn't been in contact for years and she had just got back from a very long trip with her whole family, four kids, around Europe in a campervan. We immediately said "Wow, that's the solution we've been waiting for! That would suite us perfectly! That's what we'll to do!" So it started with the desire, even though we didn't yet know exactly how we would make it work. Then, one day, we stumbled onto a solution when we heard about someone else's travels and how they had done it. Everything was suddenly crystal clear for us. We got the perfect answers to our "how to travel" and off we went...

A. How to Travel - What Would You Like to DO?

What do you want your trip to be like? This can require some thought, unless you're the totally spontaneous type who just turns the key in the door and says "OK, I'm off, I'll see where I end up and what happens".

You can do it this way if you like. You don't need to think about what you want to do, or how you want to travel and stay. But it can be good to do some planning around what you leave behind if you want to avoid things like unexpected bills showing up and ruining your trip....

The rest of us may want to consider these things a bit before we step out of the door though.

So, what kind of person are you? What's your dream travel scenario? Where have you always wanted to go? What have you been longing to do?

How do you like to spend your time? What do you feel really happy doing?

Do You Like Adventure?

A bit at least we assume, or you wouldn't be reading this! Are you longing for some action and adrenaline rushes and opportunities to challenge your limits? Do activities like river rafting, mountain climbing, heliskiing and driving around a desert in a 4-wheel drive give you that happy excited feeling?

Maybe You Prefer a More Spiritual Path?

Do things like going on a retreat, visiting a meditation center or a place like Taizé in the South of France feel like something you've been longing to do?

A friend of ours went to a Buddhist center in Nepal for three months and had the time of her life.

Another friend walked the pilgrimage El Camino in southern Spain and at the same time wrote a book about it.

Do You Have a Special Passion or Hobby You Want to Pursue and Could Build Your Trip Around?

Are you an avid dancer and would love to learn Flamenco in southern Spain or Tango in Buenos Aires?

We followed our children's passion for the Lord of the Rings and planned a stay in New Zealand around that. Got a "LOTR guide book to NZ" to help and inspire us. We visited lots of places where they shot the film. We even filmed our own version of Gollum crawling in the river with Aron, the youngest, acting as Gollum in the freezing water. We found the exact place, even recognized the rocks from the movie! We also met with people who'd been in the crew (we really enjoyed hearing all the stories!) We had such a great time and of course couldn't avoid doing a lot more than "just" LOTR things. We took the opportunity to visit old relatives as well as many homeschooling families, we experienced the fantastic scenery as well as the Maori culture and last but not least, learned about the most boring sport we've ever seen – cricket (sorry cricket lovers). Well, maybe we just didn't learn enough about it …

Would You Love to Spend Time Out in Nature?

To be in the great outdoors around the world, doing field trips and experiencing new and different landscapes, plants and animals, is that something that makes your heart sing? What kind of surroundings would you like to experience – jungles, savannah, the arctic, oceans?

Our close friend Gabi has a passion for two things, the ocean and photography. She travels the world together with her husband Gunter and their 3 children, spending their time on beaches, islands and at sea around the world taking the most amazing photos. That's when she and the rest of the family really enjoy life the most.

Maybe You Want to Take the Opportunity and Use Your Long Term Trip to Get in Better Health and Shape?

Are you attracted to doing physical things like hiking, canoeing, biking, or swimming? Maybe do a "jog around the world" tour? Or spend time at a health centre (as a guest or a volunteer) and learn how to take better care of yourself and start that new, healthy-living life?

Do You Want to Explore Different Cultures Around the World?

Indulge in what different countries or cultures have to offer. Maybe learn to cook in France? Study Shakespeare in England? Learn more about original inhabitants, like the Aborigines in Australia or the Sami people in Northern Scandinavia?

One of our neighbors went on a nine month motor biking tour around Scotland and learned how to play the bag pipes and also studied more about his other big interest - Whisky!

Do You Want to Spend Time Improving a Skill?

Do you have a specific skill you want to improve or even learn from scratch? A new language? Does an idea like traveling to Spanish speaking countries around the world and return home speaking a new language excite you? Take classes, maybe stay with Spanish speaking families and really get into your new language? We've actually had an American visitor who spent time here in Sweden to learn Swedish. While staying with us, as well as with other families, he helped out with different things in exchange for Swedish "lessons" (the kids read children books in Swedish to him among other things☺) and food and shelter.

You Could Use Your Journey to Connect or Reconnect With Relatives or Old Friends Around the World.

Maybe you have some great friends who moved that you'd love to see again? Or relatives you've heard lots about but have never met. Older people you want your children to meet (and meet yourself) while there's still time…We made a tour through Europe once when we visited every thinkable old (and new) friend. It took us some months and we even had to take some "time off" from all the socializing now and then, but it was a great way to strengthen the bonds to our friends.

Do You Want to Travel Around the World and Earn Money at the Same Time?

You could set up an internet business before you leave, learn about travel writing and share with others about your trip. Dance around the world like Matt from www.wherethehellismatt.com. Create your own unique theme around your specific "skill," and maybe a sponsor will turn up and pay for your long term journey. Or travel around the world and collect new ideas for a business that you can start when you get back home or get new inspiration for a business you already have.

Here we are inclined to remember a British couple, Chris & Carolyn Caldicott who traveled around the world trying new exciting food wherever they went, collecting the recipes and taking photos of the different local dishes. They then made their own cook books –"World Food Cafe" and started a vegetarian restaurant in London with the same name where they serve dishes from around the world. So we guess whenever they felt up for another journey they just had to come up with a new book idea. They combined their interest and talents to make something more out of their journeys than just visiting and seeing places.

So What Interests or Talents Do You Have That You Can Build Your Journey Around?

To have a main theme can be of help if you're not sure what you want your trip to look like or if you loose yourself in all the alternatives that exist. If you read travel magazines, watch travel programs, listen to other travelers and find that everything you see and hear sounds just great (or maybe nothing of what you see or hear suits you) then it can be a bit frustrating. And even if it's a good idea to find inspiration outside of yourself, it's crucial to also go within and take a look at who you are as a person and see what really resonates with you.

Whatever you choose to do during your extended world travel, just be open to wherever it takes you and the experiences it gives you and remember, there are no right or wrong ways.

Also, try not to cram too much into your trip, it's not supposed to be a substitute for your job!

And another important thing: whatever you want to do but don't have time to do this time, you can always do the next!

And remember: anything can be an excuse to travel!

Network Travel, a Social Way to Travel - Interact with People, Feel more like a Local than a Tourist, and Stay for Free

Network Traveling is a way to travel based on your own personal contacts or contacts through an organization.

It's a social way of traveling that allows you to meet, connect and interact with many different people.

You stay for a very low cost, often for free, and you get the opportunity to experience the world as a local rather than just a tourist.

Personal Network Traveling

Our daughters are passionate letter writers and have pen pals all over the world. A few years ago, they really wanted to meet with their two oldest letter-writing friends, who live in the USA and Canada.

We contacted their families and they invited us all to come and stay with them! It was a great experience for the girls to meet their pen pals and we all had some fantastic weeks together with these people we'd heard so much about over the years.

Having traveled so far, we wanted to take the opportunity to see a bit more of this part of the world. Through our pen pal families, we were then introduced to their friends, who in turn introduced us to their friends and they all invited us to come and stay. We stayed with one family for three whole weeks!

We traveled in this way, staying with different families, for three months, all the way from Michigan to Seattle and up to British

Columbia, Canada and we didn't spend one dollar for accommodation since nobody allowed us to pay.

We got so many invitations we could easily have continued to travel for another three months (or more)!

Another time we were traveling to New Zealand, and since it was our first time there we didn't know anyone. The first thing we did when we started to plan the trip, was to join some different New Zealand Home Schooling groups on the internet. We told them we were a Swedish family who planned to go to NZ and we were looking for people to meet with and places to stay.

Soon, we had several invitations from these friendly Kiwis to come and visit. They lived all over both islands. From the furthest north to the most southern parts (whatever is north and south down there).

Some people invited us to come and visit for a day, others to stay for a longer time. Since we felt we wanted some "privacy," as well as a way to transport ourselves around to all these places, we decided to rent a campervan. With our rolling home we then went from family to family and stayed on their land, in their garden or yard and we didn't spend one New Zealand Dollar on campsites or hotels or any other kind of accommodation. But, apart from the financials, the most fantastic thing about traveling like this is all the people you get to meet, share your different stories with, learn from and become friends with.

We are also open to helping people who contact us in the same way. We have had visitors from all over the world come to stay. Or we have found somewhere for them to stay in another part of Sweden (it's actually a big country, but almost empty of people). Or we have met and guided them around in our beautiful capital or just connected in some other way.

Now and then we get contacted by people who at some point have invited us to stay and now they themselves have been inspired to travel and are ready to come and visit us instead. This can often be as fun as traveling yourself, and you get a chance to give back!

We all have plenty of connections, but usually don't think this can be part of making a travel dream come true. Our experience is that people around the world are usually very open to, and interested in meeting with people with whom they share a common interest. We have traveled, and also stayed for free, for months like this, visiting new friends.

Consider for a moment your own networks. You may think that you don't have any, but consider:

- Your immediate and extended family
- Your interests and hobbies
- Your work
- Your friends and extended friends
- Your children's school and their friends
- Your church, your neighbors, your old classmates...

There's an abundance of ways to create your dream trip. Just think about your interests and the people you know. From there you can make all kinds of connections to travel around the world!

"A journey is best measured in friends, rather than miles."
– Tim Cahill

Organized Network Traveling

Another way you can travel is by joining an organization which provides the travel network for you. You can then travel around and use the contacts within the organization to connect with people and stay for free. Some of the most well known organizations are:

• Servas

• WWOOF (World Wide Opportunities on Organic Farms)

• Couch Surfing

• Hospitality Club

• Women Welcome Women World Wide

• Helpx

• Stay4free

These organizations take different forms. Some of them require that you help out a few hours a day in exchange for free food and a place to sleep. It can be all kinds of work, farm work, garden work, building, cooking, baby sitting, helping children with homework, you name it. These places usually allow you, and want you to stay for a bit longer – weeks or even months. A couple of examples of these organizations are WWOOF and Helpx.

Other Organized Network Travel groups only allow you to stay a few days but you are not required to do any special work in exchange. Some examples of these are Servas and Couchsurfing.

When we ourselves have traveled with a hospitality organization, it has mostly been through WWOOF – in Europe and especially Spain. We have many great memories of these stays but one special place comes to our minds, Los Arenalejos in the mountains above Marbella, southern Spain. The family who runs this huge farm is now dear friends to us and we have stayed there several times, helping out with various things. They grow almost everything on their land, for example olives (hundreds and hundreds of old trees), avocados (almost as much), oranges, mandarins, lemons, grapefruits, apricots, peaches, apples, pears, pecans, and almonds to name a few, so there's always something to do. One of the highlights is when we helped out with the olive harvest. We collected olives for days, took it to "El Molino", the mill, where they cold pressed the olives into this fantastic oil which we then brought loads of back to Sweden. The best oil ever!

The number of hospitality travel organizations is increasing all the time. More people are realizing how valuable it can be, not only to stay for free, but also to connect with people from other parts of the world (or even from the same part) both as travelers and as hosts.

Be a Visitor or a Host

A few years ago, we visited a family in a very rural part of New Zealand (you know it is rural when the post boat only comes once a week!). They live and work at this extremely beautiful place, with dolphins swimming in the bay, farming clams, breeding sheep and cows and renting out cottages.

At first it seemed very isolated to us, but we soon realized they lived a much more social and international life than most people. They were hosts for some different hospitality travel organizations and had visitors from all (yes, ALL) over the world. We know, we actually read their guest books and even found visitors from Sweden.

People came and stayed for different lengths of time and they received food and shelter in exchange for helping with whatever needed to be done or stayed as a paying guest.

We have also had visitors come to us through WWOOF. We especially remember a man who came on his bike from England. He didn't take the quickest route but made a small detour around France and Italy first. He was a great help with repairing things around the house.

Another time we had a young man from New York come to spend time with our kids and to "teach" them English. They very much ended up teaching each other different things though, since they taught him things like harvesting honey, chopping wood and Swedish.

We've also had a family staying at our home for a whole winter when we were traveling ourselves. They were a Finnish-English couple with a son and they had actually been WWOOFing themselves around the world for five years as a family!

As you see, you can use a hospitality travel organization both as a traveler and as a host. This way of traveling is about both giving and receiving. When you travel, you get support in different ways. You also give friendship as well as share of yourself and teach people about your part of the world. You can also give in the form of being open to letting people contact you when they are away from their home.

We would love to see more people use this way to travel and build relationships around the world! Network Travel really makes the world shrink. It helps you feel at home wherever you go and if you don't go but stay at home, you can be connected to the rest of the world by letting people come and visit you. And you can build a network that you can travel in yourself if you one day change your mind and want to go for some adventure too. Network Travel also makes you feel safer – you learn that you have friends everywhere! In short, Network Travel really makes the world a better place!

So, again, think for a moment about your own social connections and remember, it's actually only your thinking (or not thinking) that sets the limit on what's possible to do and how it's possible to travel!

Volunteering

Volunteering is about traveling and making a difference. It's about sharing who you are and what you have with those who are less fortunate.

It's also about traveling the world and at the same time be part of making it a better place.

There's a multitude of ways that you can contribute by volunteering while you travel. Imagine for example if you could:

- Help to build houses for underprivileged families in Kenya
- Monitor lions and other wild animals in South Africa
- Teach children to read in Vietnam
- Rehabilitate animals in the rainforest in Costa Rica
- Take care of orphans in Eastern Europe
- Teach English in Argentina
- Help with medical care in India

These are actually things that you could be doing, and places you could spend time in while traveling the world. There are lots of other places and activities where your help as a volunteer would be much appreciated.

Hiking in Arizona, a sunny, hot and dry experience

In Murwillumbah, Australia by contrast, it was this green and lush!

Victorian Ball in San Diego. Traveling takes you in many new directions!

At a seminar with Mark Viktor Hansen and Jack Canfield in Los Angeles

What Can I Give?

If you have ever asked yourself questions like "What can I give?" rather than "What can I get?" – This is definitely something you may want to consider.

Volunteering is about donating your time and energy, your knowledge and experience. We promise you that what you get back will be so profound it will change your life forever. And even if your aim is to give, you will probably get just as much back.

Traveling and making a difference by doing community work can be done in many different ways and in many different fields: medical care, reforestation, construction, office work, teaching, and computer programming to name a few.

You can participate in programs for just a few weeks up to months or even years. You can volunteer and stay under more primitive conditions, as well as stay in refined hotels and help out in all kinds of ways during daytime.

You Will be Part of the Solution...

When you volunteer, you are part of a movement that supports the good and helps the world to move forward in positive directions. By volunteering you will contribute to make changes for the better as well as:

- Learn all kinds of new skills
- Get opportunities to experience new and local communities
- Gather unique travel experiences
- Contribute to your host and host community
- Make lots of new friends
- Become re-energized and get a new perspective
- Get credentials to put on your job or student resume

You will realize it's so much more fulfilling to DO something to help create a better existence than to just sit around and be overwhelmed by all the negative information from the media and from your surroundings.

But maybe most important of all, as a Traveling Volunteer, you are part of creating solutions, rather than creating problems!

"We ourselves feel that what we are doing is just a drop in the ocean. But the ocean would be less because of that missing drop."
- Mother Teresa

B. What Means of Transport Will Suit You Best?

How you would like to travel is of course related to where you want to go and what you want to do.

Transportation may be something you just want to consider for taking you from one place to another. It can also be where you want to put the main focus for your whole trip.

"Remember what Bilbo used to say: It's a dangerous business Frodo, going out your door. You step onto the road, and if you don't keep your feet, there's no knowing where you might be swept off to."
- J.R.R Tolkien

Walking

Do you love walking? Would you consider making some, or all, of your trip on foot?

We have some friends, a Swedish family, who put everything they needed (and the youngest of their five children) into a couple of bike trailers and then walked all the way from Sweden to England. When the arrived there, they continued to explore the country by foot before they went back to Sweden. We assume they never got jet lag and they will probably remember their trip for the rest of their lives.

Another example is Rosie Swale-Pope, who, on her fifty seventh birthday decided to take herself around the world - by running! The whole trip took her almost five years and she says it was so worth it. She also said:

"Running can take you to places that do not exist if you travel in any other way. Maybe even more than walking, because you can get so exhausted, almost fail every so often, and are vulnerable and shaky. Sometimes when you are weakest, you can feel things the most strongly. This is when those you meet in the midst of their own difficult lives and situations, are not fearful of you. You're treading gently through someone else's land, part of the life going on all around you. Part of the people, places, sunrises, storms, terrors and joys; seeing, feeling, laughing, crying, in happiness or despair."

Cycling

Some Canadian friends of ours took the whole family, six people, cycling around Europe for six months. They started out in England and then cycled to Ireland, Belgium, Holland, France and Germany. They even visited us in Sweden but as we are at the border of the polar circle and their time was limited, they actually took the plane to visit us and to see a bit of this terrific country.

Another example is the American Sahtre-Vogel family with two boys who, as we write this, are going from Alaska to the very south of South America by bike. They plan the trip to take a year and a half and a while ago when we spoke to them, they had reached as far as Quito, the capital of Ecuador.

Motorcycling

Motorcycling is another option which is a big dream for many people. Motorcycling often represents the ultimate freedom, and to also combine that with the freedom of long term traveling can be a terrific adventure. We have been following Ewan McGregor and Charley Boorman's travels around the world on film and in books and we have to admit it can feel tempting, even for such non-motorcyclists as we are.

Driving

We have traveled a lot by car ourselves, sometimes towing a trailer, sometimes not, at other times with a campervan. Even if this doesn't give you as much time to appreciate the landscape and scenery as walking or cycling, it does give you the opportunity to see lots of things and the freedom to just stop wherever you want or follow that interesting road you just discovered. It also allows you to bring all those things you need for your trip that you consider absolutely necessary, and which you are surprised to find when you get back and think "why on earth did I bring this?"

Train

To some people, train is *the* way to travel.

We have a friend whose whole life is about trains. He travels on them, takes pictures of them and makes films about them. He talks about them – all the time. You don't need to be a train lover to this extent to find advantages in this form of transportation. We love traveling by train too. You just sit there and look at the different landscapes you're passing. Or read a book. Or talk to fellow travelers. Or eat, sleep or do some writing. Or maybe even some wine tasting which we did on the Empire Builder in the USA when we traveled from Chicago to Seattle for forty six hours.

Boat

We dream a lot about sailing and traveling the world by boat, but it's still a dream we haven't turned into reality.

Many others have though. And if you are a passionate sailor, this is probably an alternative you have already considered. Apart from sailing around the world, there are many options if you're tempted to travel on the water.

A friend of ours got a job cooking on a cargo ship. She was even allowed to bring all her five children! They were going to go around the world on this ship for a year but in the end illness intervened and the trip was cancelled but we thought it really sounded like a fantastic idea!

"If it's an experience you're after then cargo ship travel may be just your cup of tea; think whale watching from the bridge, celestial star gazing at midnight, and late night dance offs with a big fat engineer called Viktor. What more could you ask for?"
- Kate from loco2travel.com

Flying

When you talk about traveling, most people associate it with flying. To reach distant destinations it is easy to go by plane. And for long distances, it's the most common way of course. But you don't have to use it all the time. You can do long distances by plane and then get around on that new continent or in that new country by some other means of transportation.

Although there are problems to be solved with all the flying that we do, it is a fantastic way to have the chance to see the world and meet with its people. Use it with awareness and combine it with other great ways to get around as it suits you.

Surface Travel or Slow Travel

A while ago, we interviewed Ed Gillespie. Ed traveled around the world together with his girlfriend Fiona, for a whole year – without flying.

During their twelve plus month's trip they used many different modes of transport, including a few cargo ships, trains and busses, to take them around the globe. Their journey took them all the way from the UK, through Europe, Russia, China, and Japan where they took their first cargo ship over to NZ. They continued over to Australia, and from there they did their first trans-oceanic crossing over to Baja,

California. Finally, a last sea crossing from Costa Rica back to Europe. And all this traveling was done without ever boarding a plane!

They had several reasons for choosing this today a bit different way to travel the world. They did not want to contribute to huge carbon damages in the climate and they wanted to allow themselves to experience a more intimate relationship with different people, cultures and landscapes. We think Ed expresses it best himself. On his blog, www.lowcarbontravel.com, he says that:

"It is all about a rediscovery of the joys of slow travel; the transition of landscape, people, culture and language, of traveling through rather than just over countries, of a realization that holidays can start the minute you leave your front door not the moment you arrive at your destination".

We think this feels very tempting and even though we have traveled quite a lot ourselves without flying, we have never actually traveled around the world like this – yet!

Use your imagination

Apart from these more popular ways to travel, there are all kinds of ways that people use to take themselves off in different directions. One family we have known for many years are planning to build a carriage to put behind their horses and travel through Europe in that. We also just heard of a German family of six who are, at this moment, doing a four month hike with a donkey across the Alps.

We even heard about some people who were actually swimming around the world!

So, what kind of person are you?

Does putting on a backpack and just walk away sound like the most horrid nightmare you can imagine, or does it awaken a feeling of freedom and excitement within you?

Could taking your bike be the perfect way for you to get in shape at the same time as you practice living your life at a slower pace?

Does putting your family into a campervan and just start driving sound like a dream come true, or would this be one of the worst scenarios you could imagine?

Whatever means you dream of using to take yourself around the world, or part of the way, there are a multitude of variations to accomplish it. There's even a big chance someone else has done it already, someone you can learn from to make your trip both easier and better.

To think and fantasize about this can help you get a clearer picture of what kind of person you are and what would be the perfect way for you to travel.

And, however you choose to go, enjoy the journey, and remember:

It's not only about arriving at the destination – It's also about enjoying the process of getting there…

C. Where to Stay – Travel and Accommodation

Is accommodation an important issue for you or is it totally unimportant where you spend your nights (and days) when you travel? Do you want to let circumstances decide where you spend the night or do you want to have everything planned for the whole trip?

As with transportation, where to stay can be just an impulsive, unplanned, minor detail of your trip or, it can be something that your whole journey is based upon. It can be something you choose to spend the biggest part of your travel budget on, or you may want it to be something you put as little money into as possible.

Depending on where you want to go and what you want to do, there are a number of different ways to solve the accommodation issue when you're on the road.

Hotels

Long gone are the days when most people considered hotel stays as the only option when you are on the road. Furthermore, when you travel for extended periods, you usually don't want (or can't afford) to stay in hotels every day.

There may be days or periods when you want to choose the convenience and comfort of a hotel though. When we were in India for example, rather exhausted after having been traveling around the world for several months, we took a break from everything and checked into a luxury hotel for a few days. Even in a country like that, 5 star hotels are not super cheap, but compared to western prices, they can be rather affordable. Whether you choose a local, economy style accommodation or a five star internationally recognized hotel chain is of course an individual preference, but it's useful to know that local accommodations are usually a bit tricky to find on the internet.

Often, smaller, private family hotels and inns don't have computerized booking systems and you may have to look around when you arrive at a place or go to the tourist information office.

There are many excellent sites on the internet where you can book hotels worldwide or just surf around and see what's available and what the costs are. There are also lots of travel forums where you can find other travelers' tips on accommodations around the world as well as ask for help and advice.

Hostels

Hostels are much cheaper than hotels and you usually have the opportunity to prepare your own meals (and sometimes do your laundry as well). A hostel is also a place where it is easy to meet other travelers and share your travel experiences.

You can choose from slightly more costly private rooms to cheaper rooms with many beds. Hostels are not very common outside of the first world though.

We have stayed in hostels quite a lot, especially when the kids were young. It was a practical solution with the opportunity to bring our own food and cook and there's often some kind of "living room" so it can be a bit more "homey" than a hotel. Hostels are sometimes placed in fun and different places and we have stayed on a big ship, an old train as well as in an old prison (where you could come and go as you want though).

Home stays

Staying in people's private houses when you travel is very common mainly in countries outside of the first world. People have a spare room that they offer to travelers and you can stay there at a low cost and be like a member of the family. If you don't feel like being that social, there are home stays that are more of the "Bed and Breakfast" kind.

A home stay is a perfect way to really connect with local people and also to support their own small tourist business.

You learn more about the area you're in and its culture and it's also a perfect way to learn a new language if that's what you're interested in.

Renting

Renting a house or an apartment is always a possibility, especially if you plan stay in the same area for an extended time.

When we rent a place, we usually want to check it out and get a feel for the area first, so when we look into renting we normally contact real estate agents when we arrive someplace.

Other people prefer to have everything settled when they arrive and you can of course search for places and settle everything over the internet in advance.

Sometimes you don't want to pay the whole cost of the rental by yourself and then one idea is of course to find someone to share the house or apartment with.

A good idea is also always to travel "off season". You'll then have a greater supply of available renting units and it's easier to find places at a discounted price.

As with finding local hotels, private places for rent often aren't connected to a computerized system and then you cannot book in advance. This most often means that you'll have to look around for them when you arrive. Tourist offices, real estate agencies and local news papers are some places to look for long term renting accommodations.

There are some bigger organizations where you can book in advance if you prefer to be safe and plan ahead, but they can sometimes be a bit pricier.

You can also use www.craigslist.org for local classifieds and forums for over fifty countries around the world. On Craig's List you can find housing, services, jobs - well, just about everything.

Camping (Trailer, Campervan or Tent)

If you are going to be traveling around a lot, one option is to rent or buy a car and a trailer or a campervan and then stay at campsites or wherever you feel like along the way (wherever that is allowed). Depending on your comfort level, you can choose from really big, luxurious, fully-equipped trailers or campervans to small ones that just provide you with a bed and something to cook on.

Traveling like this gives you a lot of freedom to explore different places and at the same time you have your "home" and all your stuff with you.

When our children were younger, we did a lot of traveling this way and we found it absolutely perfect. Always having their stuff with us and always being able to just stop to make food. It's a big advantage when you travel like this, that whatever new places and circumstances you are in, you always have your own "home" and familiar things around you if things get a bit too adventurous or overwhelming (which they certainly can when you're on the road).

And if you're a bit more willing to forego a few comforts, you can also travel with a tent. And if you think you can give up the car, you could be really adventurous and choose a bike and a tent.

Network Traveling

To travel within a Network, either your own, through your friends, family, interests, or hobbies or through some Hospitality Exchange organization, are other options.

See Network Traveling for more information about this alternative.

A variation of Network traveling is alternative- or eco villages that exist in many places around the world. Often, they are open to and interested in promoting their way of living and have a place for people to come and stay for shorter or longer periods. You can sometimes stay for free as a volunteer and help out, or as a paying guest and support the economy of the village.

House Swapping

Swapping your home with another family somewhere in the world is a great way to stay for free, live in a real home and experience a place more like a local than as a tourist or traveler. At the same time, there's someone taking care of your own home and watering your plants.

We haven't done any house swapping ourselves (yet). We planned to at one stage but something came up and our plans fell through.

We had many very interesting offers to choose from at that time, from a cottage on the grounds of the huge Palace of Versailles outside Paris, France, to a bungalow on the beach in the Caribbean. And that for a house in "un-exotic" Sweden!

House Sitting

Another alternative to stay in a home away from home, for free, is to house sit. Here, you don't swap your home with someone else but just live in their home while they are away and maybe take care of some pets or something else that needs attention. Sometimes you even get paid.

A couple of years ago when we were going away for seven months, we needed someone to stay in our house and take care of it. Or rather, we needed someone to take care of our three cats. One of our cats we have had for a long time and it usually wasn't too difficult to find a place for him when we were away. But three were a bit more tricky to accommodate... So, just a few weeks before we left, we had an idea: we'll find a house sitter who can come and live in our home and look after it, and our cats.

So we put up an ad on a house sitting site, saying where we lived, what we wanted someone to look after especially (our precious cats) and how long we were going to be away for.

We must admit we didn't have much hope to find someone willing to spend a whole winter in Sweden. To our big surprise though, the answers came pouring in! It looked like people from all over the world were interested in experiencing some ice and snow. We were particularly surprised to find so many Australians willing to exchange their summer for the Swedish winter!

Anyway, we finally decided to invite a Canadian/American couple with a baby to come and stay. The mother had actually been a house sitter for seven years (!) taking care of people's houses in different parts of the world and worked as a writer at the same time! A perfect combination!

So they came and we left. We both got what we were looking for, and everything worked out perfectly. If you're looking for a way to travel the world and stay in one place for a period of time (it doesn't have to be for months, you can house sit for shorter periods too) or if you want somebody to take care of your home when you are traveling yourself, we highly recommend that you check out this alternative.

As we started off by saying, traveling does absolutely not have to equal staying in hotels (unless that's what you prefer of course). There are lots of alternatives to choose from and today, the internet makes finding people to connect with, and ways to stay, so much easier than it used to be.

D. And, Last But Not Least, Where Would You Like To Go?

Often, this is the question many people start out with when they consider traveling and for some, the answer is clear. Others don't have a specific destination connected to their travel dream.

"For my part, I travel not to go anywhere, but to go. I travel for travel's sake. The great affair is to move."
— Robert Louis Stevenson

How about you? Do you want to do some extended travel and go to the other side of the world? Or just "as far away as possible?" Or "anywhere," as long as it's a new place you've never visited? Maybe you'd love to travel within your own country, or one that's really close?

When you start to think about extended travel, you realize that the options are endless. Even today, when the internet has made the world shrink, it's still a big place.

Asking other people about where to go can give you some ideas, but it can as well be of no help at all. You're not them. They have their dream scenarios and needs, you have yours. So what do you dream to see? What are you longing to experience?

What would it say on the departure screen you would be staring at as you prepare to take off for your dream destination?

Would you even be at an airport? Maybe you'd be standing on a train station? Or waiting for a ship to take you away? Or mounting your new, fully packed bike?

To think about these questions can really help you to get into that travel mood. At least that's the case for us. As soon as we start fantasizing about where we want to go next, ideas, as well as solutions on how to manage challenges that undoubtedly turn up, start to flow.

When we start to think and talk about our next dream trip, we're as good as on our way.

Also, when we're talking about extended travel – of being away from home for a long period of time – we all have different views on what that looks like.

For some people, traveling for three months, six months, a year or more, is all about visiting lots of different places around the world. For this group, long term travel is really about the "travel" part. You want to travel around and experience as many different areas and cultures as possible and expose yourself to new impressions all the time.

For others, it's more about staying for a longer period in one or a few places somewhere away from home. Those who are into this version of extended travel may be more interested in living an "everyday" life in a new surrounding different to your normal one and go deeper into that area and that culture.

So, where would you like to go?

Find out how you want to travel

We encourage you to really take a look at these different areas of traveling, what to do, where to go, where to stay and how to get there. This will help you get a clearer picture of what you want your long journey to look like. Really get into it and immerse yourself with pictures and ideas about every facet of your dream scenario. Don't get caught in your old Buts - just imagine if you could choose exactly the way you wanted everything to be, what would it be like? Start to do this NOW, and we promise you, you'll have taken the first steps on your amazing journey!

7. Some Final Thoughts

During the last 15 years our whole family has made 7 trips of 6 months or longer. Again and again, we have set off for our journeys only to come back full of new energy and inspiration. Each travel experience has also given us many insights and ideas about how we want to live and how we can improve things. We've often come back with solutions to "problems" we've had before we left and, most of the time, we don't even see them as a challenge any more.

Every time we've started to think about and plan a new trip, we've encountered a great number of Buts. From not enough money and not enough time to the fear of flying. Some of the obstacles have been rather easy to get over, whereas others have resurfaced again and again (and still do). Every single one of these times though, we have managed to overcome whatever obstacles we have been facing and been able to set off on our travels. And boy, are we ever glad we did!

And we want to point this out, that even if we've taken a few long term trips at this stage, we still have this little voice in our heads telling us what we can't do and how impossible things really are. It does require some focus and commitment to take ourselves past them. But that's actually all there is. And it's the same for you. We assume that, if you've read this far, you're really interested in taking the leap and going on that long journey. We also guess that you already have encountered at least a couple of reasons why it will be difficult, or even impossible in your case. What we want you to remember though, is that you are not unique. It's the same for everyone who's considering taking a big step. It's the same for us as well as all the travelers we've met along the way. We have met all kinds of travelers through the years – and we mean ALL. And if all of us can do it – we're certain that you can do it too!

As a start, we hope you have found some really good reasons to why you want to go, and what the benefits from some extended travel could be for you. Getting clear about why you really want to do this will help you so much to make it a reality.

Hopefully you have also explored a few of your own Buts - the reasons you find yourself not doing what you really want to be doing. The first step to change is to become aware of what holds you back, so don't worry if your buts seem big and overwhelming. Acknowledging that they are ruling your life is actually the first step of overcoming them!

Then there are the how to's. Maybe you're one of those who have known for years that you'd love to travel the world, you haven't just figured out how to make it possible. Or maybe you still haven't figured out the perfect way to travel. Maybe you don't need to know – you'll just throw a few things in a backpack and leave? Your ideas about how you want to travel and what you want your specific trip to look like will make it easier to take the necessary steps to create the trip you want.

The three areas, why – but – and how, are the crucial ones to get clear about when you want to take off on an adventure. Each one of them can help you gain insights into how to make your trip a reality and looking into all three will really be of big help to getting you on the road. So, however far you have come in planning your big trip, either you just got the idea when you stumbled over this book, or you have been dreaming of traveling like this for decades, you can do something today to get closer to your departure. Consider the things we've talked about and take one step (it doesn't have to be big) in the direction of where you want to go. Continue to do this every day, and we promise you, you'll soon be on your way!

And remember, to leave things behind and go out into the world for an extended period, a few months, maybe a whole year, is not a small thing. For all of us in our family, it's something that has affected our lives profoundly on every level. And when you are away exploring the world it will definitely be the same for you! After three months of travel (or six, or twelve), whether in South America, Northern Africa, Scandinavia or even in a different part of your own country, you will come back a bit - or a lot - different from who you were before you left.

After some extended travel, you will have gained more knowledge of who you are and what you want. You will have learned more about our fantastic world and most certainly you will have expanded your circle of friends, close ones as well as casual friends you've had more superficial encounters with. After some extensive traveling you will have created greater intimacy with yourself as well as with potential co- travelers and you will return home with dramatic gains in your self-esteem, confidence and self-sufficiency. You will have learned to be more fearless and to take more risks, to be a better problem solver and to adapt to different circumstances more easily than before you set off. You will be more relaxed and more experienced in living in the present and taking things as they come. You will, very likely, be a happier person!

Happy Travels and see you soon somewhere out there in this fantastic world of ours!